# Responding to Disaster

## Marty Augustine

"Success depends upon previous preparation, and without such preparation there is sure to be failure."

Confucius

# Responding to Disaster

# Introduction

A disaster can happen anywhere, at any time...
Are you prepared?

Many public safety officers are unaware of the many dangers that lurk in our everyday lives. Life threatening hazards are all around us. Severe weather, hazardous materials, terrorism, accidents, fires...The list goes on and on. No jurisdiction is immune from disaster. Odds are good that you will encounter a disaster or hazardous situation at some time in your career.

***It's not a matter of if a disaster will strike, but when.***

Some disasters may offer advance warning, others may strike without warning. How you prepare and how you respond may be the difference between life and death. The purpose of this book is to provide you with the basic concepts of emergency preparedness and an awareness of the hazards involved with disaster response. Admitting and accepting that *you* could become a victim is the first step in preparedness.

This book will guide you through the complex world of disasters. The responsibility of emergency planning and preparedness is shared by all. Survival is in your hands...

Content in this book is based on the emergency preparedness guide **At Ground Zero** by Marty Augustine. Material also corresponds with Marty's Responding to Disaster seminars.

# Chapter 1

## Disasters throughout History

What is a disaster? A disaster is any event that causes disruption, harm or destruction. Earthquakes, tornadoes, blizzards, hurricanes, floods, chemical spills, disease pandemics and terrorist attacks are all real threats that can affect any of us, regardless of who you are or where you live. "It won't happen to me" or "it won't happen here" are probably the most common misconceptions about disaster planning and response. Many have the belief that disasters can only occur in certain places. If you are not in those areas, you'll be safe. Unfortunately, this is not true. A major catastrophe could occur anywhere, at any time. Disasters cause billions of dollars in damage annually, not to mention the emotional toll. Anyone can be the victim of a disaster.

There are two main types of disasters, natural and man-made. Natural disasters include weather and other naturally occurring events. Earthquakes, tornadoes, thunderstorms, snow storms, ice storms, flooding, etc. are all natural. Man-made disasters are things such as terrorist attacks, chemical spills, industrial accidents and vehicle related accidents. Disease pandemics and fires can fall into either category. The breakout of diseases can occur naturally but they can also be spread by malicious intent through human caused acts of terrorism. Fires can be man-made or caused by a natural event such as lightning.

Disasters are nothing new. Catastrophic events can be traced back to biblical times, the days of the dinosaurs, the ice age and beyond. The Earth is in a constant state of change. Our planet has been molded by nature throughout time. The Earth is far different now than it was long ago.

Continents have shifted, mountains have risen, climates have changed and societies have been wiped out. We as humans are just a small speck on the historical time line of the world.

During our short time here, humans and animals have simply learned to adapt to the changes presented. These changes will surely continue long after humans are gone. Although we have done a fairly good job of overcoming many of the things presented to us, life is very fragile. It can all be taken away at any time.

There are accounts of natural disasters going back thousands of years, but good weather data records have only been kept since about the late 1800's. Prior to that time there were not very many ways of measuring things such as wind speed, earthquake intensity, tornado size and other data. Communication between widespread areas was limited and delayed. Accurate data was surely lost in many occasions.

In the days of westward expansion in the United States, thousands of people died trying to make their way across the country. These brave settlers faced unimaginable hazards and hardships on their journeys. There was no way of forecasting weather conditions and most were unaware of what dangers would be encountered on the trails. Settlers were often stranded in extreme cold or brutal heat without proper supplies. They had to endure nearly every type of weather condition, as well as other hazards such as sickness, attackers and robberies. Many had to turn back or try to survive with what they had. Unfortunately, many did not survive. With thousands of people in the uninhabited wilderness of early America, there was no way of tracking everyone who died. Those who did survive were either lucky, or prepared.

Things have changed a lot since then, but one thing stays the same - We are always surrounded by danger. How you prepare will determine your outcome. You can't rely on others...

Most people are aware of the dangers of natural threats, but not all disasters are naturally occurring. Boats can sink, airplanes, trains and other vehicles can crash. Cities can be and have been destroyed by explosions, fires and industrial accidents. Hazardous chemicals are a normal part of our society. There are many potential hazards we often overlook in our normal duties.

We've all worked accidents involving vehicles, but did you ever stop to think about what those vehicles were carrying?

Terrorism is a current threat, but it has been a danger throughout time. Homeland security has now become a common term in our lives. It's also a major part of the emergency planning and response process as new threats surface daily. Threats we once knew as being far away have now come to our front door.

Many citizens believe our society is safe from disasters because the government will be there to rescue everyone from anything that may occur. Although the best possible effort is being made, we know public safety providers simply can't protect everyone all the time. In an era of budget cuts and limited resources, staffing and equipment is being stretched thin. Because of this, it is critical that we learn to provide a more *efficient* and *effective* response. Responders have a duty to protect and serve the entire jurisdiction they are employed by, but ultimately each individual citizen is responsible for their own safety and security.

The public expects a quality public safety response, but how we can this be accomplished with limited resources?  In the event of a major disaster, emergency workers will be overwhelmed. Emergency preparedness is cooperative effort. The public must be involved in the planning process in order to affect a better response. This is an often overlooked aspect of public safety.

Our society has become too reliant on others. In our modern times, the response and assistance of government emergency services is often taken for granted. Things were very different before the modern days of coordinated government services. In the early days of the US government, there was no federal involvement in disaster planning or response. The government did not feel obligated to assist. Reasons for the lack of support included the small size of the US government, the centralized location of government (Washington DC) and the lack of means to provide assistance. News traveled slowly. By the time the government even found out about an incident it was probably already too late to do anything. The government did not feel it was in the best interest of the nation to get involved with disasters.

Citizens and politicians relied heavily upon the word of the constitution. There was no constitutional requirement stating the government needed to assist with disasters. Citizens did not want government involvement because they felt that is what they were trying to avoid by starting a new nation. They did not want the federal government intruding in their lives. The citizens were independent people who relied on each other for help. However, things would soon change.

In the late 1700's, the city of Portsmouth New Hampshire was a bustling port, a shipbuilding hub and a major contributor to the national economy. The city experienced two major fires in 1802 and 1805. The fires caused substantial damage, crippling the city and port. This was a major blow to the economy of the young nation. The federal government knew the city had to rebuild as soon as possible if they wanted to continue the much needed stream of revenue to the US Treasury.

The Congressional Act of 1803 is generally considered to be the first piece of federal disaster legislation. On January 22nd 1807 the US Congress authorized "all persons who, being indebted to the United States for duties on merchandise, have given bond therefor, with one, or more sureties, payable to the collector for the district of Portsmouth, in the state of New Hampshire, and who have suffered a loss of property by the late conflagration at that place, shall be and hereby are allowed to take up, or have canceled, all bonds heretofore given for duties as aforesaid, upon giving to the said collector new bonds, with one or more sureties, to the satisfaction of the said collector, for the sums of their former bonds respectively, payable in twelve months." (Source: Bills and Resolutions, House of Representatives, 9th Congress, 2nd Session Bill H.R. 40) This was very similar to the modern tax breaks used to stimulate the economy in times of trouble today. Portsmouth was rebuilt in an improved form. Better fire prevention techniques were used with the development of new construction. Streets were made wider to prevent the spread of fire and buildings were made from brick rather than wood to prevent future fires. Emergency planning was being born.

This was one of the first examples of disaster mitigation in America. These fires also provoked legislation mandating building codes to further ensure safety. In the century that followed, ad hoc legislation was passed more than 100 times in response to other disasters.

President Herbert Hoover commissioned the Reconstruction Finance Corporation in the 1930's when the federal approach to problems was becoming more popular. The commission was given authority to make disaster loans for repair and reconstruction of certain public facilities following an earthquake, and later, other types of disasters.

In 1934, the Bureau of Public Roads was given authority to provide funding for highways and bridges damaged by natural disasters. The Flood Control Act was also passed. This gave the U.S. Army Corps of Engineers greater authority to implement flood control projects.

In the years following World War 2, Americans were becoming increasingly concerned with the threat of nuclear war. Civil Defense groups had been around since about World War 1, but they were increasing in popularity around the country during the 1950's. These groups were created to have civilians support police and fire departments by providing additional manpower in the event of an enemy attack. The primary role of civil defense was emergency preparedness. Because of the fear of nuclear attack, fallout shelters were becoming a common site in every city and town. These shelters were facilities built to protect against the threat of nuclear radiation during an attack. They were built in public buildings, schools and even some homes. They were often stocked with food and supplies. With the threat of war, people were scared. They knew they needed to prepare.

The 1950's brought about many new warnings to inform the public. Siren towers were built and radio, TV and movies presented information regarding preparedness education.

Schools became involved with emergency drills, teaching kids important safety tips such as "duck and cover".

Civil Defense remained popular until the 1980's when the threat of nuclear war lessened. The concept of Civil Defense is still around today, but it has since been integrated into more modern emergency management programs such as Community Emergency Response Teams (CERT).

In 1963, the Emergency Broadcast System went into effect. This system provided emergency warning information to citizens by television and radio. It was common to hear messages such as "This is a test. This station is conducting a test of the Emergency Broadcast System.

This is only a test" and "if this had been an actual emergency, you would have been instructed where to tune in your area for news and official information." The Emergency Broadcast System was used until 1997 when it was replaced by the Emergency Alert System (EAS). The EAS currently provides warnings for a variety of emergencies and hazards. Emergency warning technology has since progressed from radio and television to now using the internet, smart phones and text messages for notification as well. The Emergency Alert System is a critical tool for providing timely information when needed.

During the 1960's, disaster assistance was handled by the Department of Housing and Urban Development (HUD) which created the Federal Disaster Assistance Administration. The 1960s and early 1970s brought massive disasters requiring major federal response and recovery operations. Hurricane Carla struck in 1962, Hurricane Betsy in 1965, Hurricane Camille in 1969 and Hurricane Agnes in 1972. The Alaskan Earthquake hit in 1964 and the San Fernando Earthquake rocked Southern California in 1971. These events served to focus attention on the issue of natural disasters and brought about increased federal legislation.

In 1968, the National Flood Insurance Act offered new flood protection to homeowners, and in 1974 the Disaster Relief Act firmly established the process of presidential disaster declarations. The government was trying to do more to help, but emergency and disaster activities were still fragmented during these times.

When hazards associated with nuclear power plants and the transportation of hazardous substances were added to the list of natural disasters, more than 100 federal agencies were involved in some aspect of disasters, hazards and emergencies. There were also many programs at the local and state levels that had similarities to the federal programs. These programs often provided redundant services, making emergency response very inefficient.

The National Governors Association wanted to decrease the number of agencies with redundant interests because they felt it hindered federal disaster relief efforts. President Jimmy Carter was asked to centralize federal emergency functions.

President Carter issued Executive Order 12127 in 1979, merging many of the separate disaster related responsibilities into the Federal Emergency Management Agency (FEMA).

FEMA is the agency currently tasked with the federal response to disasters in the United States. The current role of FEMA is the coordination of the federal government with preparing for, preventing, mitigating the effects of, responding to, and recovering from all domestic disasters, whether natural or man-made, including acts of terrorism. The mission and activities of FEMA are best described by the organization as being the "life cycle of disaster."

Prior to FEMA, there was no single agency responsible for disaster operations. After this order, FEMA absorbed many other federal agencies. Some of the agencies merged were: the Federal Insurance Administration, the National Fire Prevention and Control Administration, the National Weather Service Community Preparedness Program, the Federal Preparedness Agency of the General Services Administration and the Federal Disaster Assistance Administration activities from HUD. Civil defense responsibilities were also transferred to the new agency from the Defense Department's Defense Civil Preparedness Agency.

In August of 1979, President Carter appointed a man named John Macy to serve as the first director of FEMA.

Macy saw the similarities between preparedness for natural hazards and Civil Defense activities and sought to merge them. FEMA began the development of an integrated emergency management system with an all-hazards approach that included "direction, control and warning systems which are common to the full range of emergencies from small isolated events to the ultimate emergency – war" (Source: FEMA History). The new agency seemed to be slowly showing improvement, but it still had a lot of work to do.

During the 1980's, the threat of nuclear war still loomed. Preparedness for a nuclear attack was still on the minds of Americans. The government was attempting to find ways to provide support to assist in the preparation of all disasters based on the suggestions of John Macy.

In November of 1988, the Robert T. Stafford Act was signed into law, amending the Disaster Relief Act of 1974. Robert T. Stafford was the 71$^{st}$ Governor of Vermont and also a state representative and Senator. Stafford was instrumental in writing and passing the law. The Stafford Act was designed as a way to promote an orderly and systemic means of federal disaster assistance to assist state and local governments. It created the system used today which triggers federal response and financial assistance after a presidential disaster declaration is made.

In its first 25 years, FEMA was faced with many unexpected events that proved emergency management could be a challenging task. Early disasters and emergencies included the Cuban refugee crisis, toxic pollution in the Love Canal in Niagara Falls, New York and a meltdown accident at the Three Mile Island nuclear power plant in Pennsylvania. The Loma Prieta, California Earthquake that occurred in 1989 and Hurricane Andrew in 1992 put FEMA in the national spotlight. The agency proved it could handle itself, but there were still problems with its operations.

In 1993, James L. Witt was nominated by President Clinton to serve as the new director of FEMA. Witt was the head of the Arkansas Office of Emergency Services. Witt was the first FEMA director to have such emergency management experience.

Upon taking office, Witt made major reforms that streamlined disaster relief and recovery operations. Emphasis was made on disaster preparedness and mitigation. He also made changes to FEMA that would allow employees to be more customer service oriented. With the cold war ending, Witt was able to redirect the limited resources of FEMA from the old civil defense methods and theories into modern relief, recovery and mitigation programs for disasters.

With the reorganization of FEMA, Congress decided to add more responsibilities to the agency. FEMA took over the management of dam safety as well as other safety tasks. The agency now focused on the four phases of emergency management: mitigation, preparation, response and recovery. This reorganization allowed the agency to better serve everyone.

President George W. Bush appointed Joe M. Allbaugh as the new director of FEMA in 2001. Only a few months after his appointment, America witnessed the terrorist attacks of September 11th, 2001.  Terrorists hijacked airplanes and flew them into the World Trade Center and Pentagon buildings. This was a major test for FEMA. No one expected or planned for the attacks we experienced. September 11th changed the way everyone looked at security and preparedness. FEMA realized it must also focus on issues of national preparedness and homeland security. The sense of security Americans once knew was suddenly taken away. The new "war on terror" had begun and America would never be the same.

Billions of dollars of new funds were directed to FEMA to help communities face the threat of terrorism. Just a few years after its 20th anniversary, FEMA was actively changing its approach toward including the new concerns of homeland security preparedness and response. New types of threats were emerging and the agency had to adapt.

In March 2003, FEMA joined 22 other federal agencies, programs and offices in becoming the Department of Homeland Security.

The new department, headed by Secretary Tom Ridge, brought a coordinated approach to national security for emergencies and disasters, both natural and man- made. The FEMA Office of National Preparedness was given the responsibility of helping to train and equip America's first responders. Many new grants were provided to aid with the response and preparedness for disasters. This included training and education as well as upgrading equipment for responders to better handles major incidents. Phrases such as "weapons of mass destruction" and "homeland security" became common terms that public safety agencies and the public needed to be prepared for. With terrorism now on the minds of the public, the threat of natural disasters seemed to take a backseat.

Everyone was reminded of natural disasters in August, 2005 when Hurricane Katrina struck Louisiana and the Gulf Coast. President Bush and FEMA faced massive public disapproval for their response to the incident. Many felt the federal response was too little and too late.

Hurricane Katrina was an example of "what can go wrong, will go wrong". Although our nation has been through many disasters, including other recent hurricanes, America had never experienced the level of disaster, rescue and recovery found with Hurricane Katrina.

The hurricane was rated as a strong category 3, a storm with sustained winds in excess of 125 miles per hour. Category 5 storms are the most intense type of hurricanes. Katrina was a Category 5 storm, but weakened slightly before coming ashore. The massive hurricane affected areas of Mississippi, Alabama, Louisiana and Florida, with southeast Louisiana being the hardest hit. Residents were given advance warning to evacuate the city but many chose not to. Even with a mandatory evacuation order being issued in New Orleans, many residents still refused to leave. An estimated 90% of residents in southeast Louisiana chose to evacuate in what was the largest mass evacuation of a major city in US history. In this large urban area, 10% of the remaining population still amounted to quite a few people.

Of those who stayed, many faced an unfortunate fate. When the storm struck, thousands of residents were stranded. Levees meant to hold back flood waters burst, causing massive flooding in the core of the city. 80% of New Orleans was underwater. Dead bodies and debris flowed in contaminated water that covered the city. Death and destruction were everywhere. Body collection did not begin for more than a week after the beginning of the storm. Over 1,800 people died as a result of the storm.

TV and radio stations went off the air. Cell phones and land line telephone service were inoperable. Roads in and out of the city were washed away. Chaos ruled the city with mass looting, robberies, murder and other crimes. Gangs took over as many police officers fled the city (it is believed a third of the New Orleans police force left). Snipers frequently shot at relief workers, rescuers and police as they worked. Helicopters were often unable to access many areas because of gunfire. New Orleans and surrounding areas were turned into a third world environment. Nearly 2 million people lost power in the areas affected.

Many residents who stayed in the city sought refuge in the Louisiana Superdome, a covered stadium. An estimated 15,000 – 20,000 people went to the Superdome for shelter. The facility rapidly filled and people had to be turned away. Many of those turned away were sent to the New Orleans Convention Center. As thousands of residents sheltered in the buildings, new problems arose. Personal belongings and people were not searched upon entering the buildings.

Weapons, alcohol and illegal drugs made their way into the shelters. There were reports of open drug use, fights, rape and general chaos. At the convention center, the building lost electricity and water pressure. Damage from the storm caused a large hole in the ceiling. Thousands were inside in dark, wet, unsanitary conditions. There were various causes of death in the shelters, but decomposing bodies were not removed. As flood waters continued to rise outside, another evacuation of the area was ordered including the Superdome. Hundreds of buses transported the evacuees to nearby areas outside of the disaster area.

Even with resources from many agencies around the nation, including the US military, the response effort was very disappointing. Recovery has since been slow for the area.

Many locations are still unusable and many residents still live in "temporary" FEMA trailers. A lesson learned from Hurricane Katrina is that preparedness is the responsibility of everyone and that we must head warnings to stay safe.

On October 4, 2006, President George W. Bush signed into law the Post-Katrina Emergency Reform Act. This act significantly reorganized FEMA, changing its response tactics, hopefully improving response to future disasters. As times change and new disasters emerge, response tactics will need to be updated and adapted. This is true not only at a national level, but also local. Agencies must continually evaluate policies, procedures and training to better serve the community.

# Chapter 2

## Historical Disasters

History has shown that no location, culture or people are immune from disaster. We can hope a major catastrophe will never happen again, but the unfortunate reality is that something will happen. History has shown us time and again that major disasters will strike.

Just because something has not occurred where you live doesn't mean that it won't. Complacency can kill. We all need to be ready for whatever comes our way. Whether it's a terrorist attack, a severe weather event or a disease outbreak, everyone should be prepared for the unexpected. There is no need to live in fear, but awareness will only serve to increase your preparedness and safety.

Although there have been thousands of known disasters throughout history, some have gathered more attention than others because of the extreme level of catastrophe. The following pages show a disaster time line. The time line demonstrates how disasters can change the way we live our lives. The intent of the list is to show the frequency of incidents and how they can happen anywhere.

This list presents only a small fraction of the lives lost in recent history during "high profile" events. It does not include acts of war and it does not include every disaster for each year listed, as hundreds of disasters occur every year. There have been many, many more natural and human caused incidents than those listed here. The lessons of our past should serve as a warning for our future. *It's not a matter of if disaster will strike, but when…*

**2011** – Joplin Missouri: An EF-5 tornado tore through the city center causing extensive damage. More than 160 deaths occurred with nearly 1,000 people injured. This storm added to the already high 2011 death toll, making this one of the deadliest severe weather years in US history.

**2011**- Tuscaloosa Alabama:  An EF-4 tornado hit the heart of the city causing over 2 Billion dollars in damage. At least 281 people were killed and thousands more injured as storms ripped through 6 southern states.

**2011** – Japan: A magnitude 9.0 earthquake caused massive damage along the east coast of Japan's main island. A resulting tsunami caused even more damage and death when it hit the coast. The combined incident caused an international nuclear scare when a nuclear reactor complex was severely damaged. The death toll may be over 10,000.

**2010** - Haiti: Exact casualties resulting from a magnitude 7 quake are still unknown, but an estimated 200,000 + people are believed to have been killed.

**2010** – Iceland: A volcanic eruption disrupted air travel around the world due to a massive ash cloud.

**2009** – Fort Hood, Texas: 13 people were killed and 30 more were wounded during a shooting rampage.

**2009** – Oklahoma: A series a tornadoes tore through the state killing 8 people, injuring a dozen more.

**2008** – Sichuan China: A magnitude 8 earthquake killed nearly 70,000 people and left more than 374,000 injured.  Over 4.8 million people were left homeless.

**2008** – Virginia: Tornadoes struck the Norfolk area injuring over 200 people. More than 140 homes were destroyed.

**2008** – New England: An ice storm left 800,000 people without electricity for several days.

**2007** – Midwest & Northeast US: A massive January winter storm moved across 9 states causing 65 storm related deaths and extensive power outages.

**2007** – Louisville, Kentucky: A freight train carrying hazardous chemicals derailed and burned causing a major evacuation. A 20 mile stretch of Interstate 65 was closed.

**2007** – Greensburg, Kansas: An EF5 tornado that measured almost 2 miles wide destroyed 95% of the town. 11 People died with many others injured. In what proved to be a test of determination, the town rebuilt as a new "green" environmentally friendly city, improving the quality of life for all who chose to remain there.

**2007** – California: 24 wildfires over a one week period killed 7 people and injured nearly 90 others. The fires burned over 516,000 acres, causing more than 500,000 residents to be evacuated.

**2007**– Blacksburg, Virginia: A student killed 32 people on the University of Virginia campus during a shooting rampage.

**2006** – Texas: In a 4 month period, wildfires burned more than 3.9 million acres. An estimated 400 homes were destroyed. More than 10,000 horses and cattle were killed as well as 11 people.

**2006** – Hawaii: A dam collapsed sending 300 million gallons of water into the valley below. Seven people were killed.

**2005** – Pakistan: A 7.6 magnitude earthquake killed over 40,000 people.

**2005** – Louisiana: More than 1,800 people were killed by Hurricane Katrina as it flooded the US Gulf Coast. Southern Louisiana was the area hardest hit. It was one of the worst hurricanes in US history.

**2004** - Indian Ocean: A tsunami caused by a 9.3 magnitude earthquake killed more than 225,000 people as it came ashore in Indonesia, Sri Lanka, India and Thailand. The earthquake had the longest faulting ever observed at the time, lasting between 8 and 10 minutes. It is one of the largest quakes ever observed on a seismograph. Resulting earthquakes were triggered as far away as Alaska.

**2004** – Beslan, Russia: Terrorists took over a school and held 1,100 people hostage. During the incident and attempted rescue, the terrorists set off bombs and engaged in a shootout killing 334 hostages.

**2003** – Southern California: Wildfires consumed more than 800,000 acres and killed 22 people.

**2003** – Worldwide: SARS (Severe Acute Respiratory Syndrome), a deadly strain of pneumonia, was responsible for nearly 400 deaths worldwide.

**2003** – West Warwick, Rhode Island: A fire caused by a pyrotechnics display caused a fire in a nightclub during a rock concert. 100 people were killed and 150 were injured.
**2002** – Central & Southeast US: A series of 70 tornadoes destroyed homes and buildings across 14 states. 36 people were killed by the storms.

**2002** – Virginia / West Virginia: A massive rain storm dumped about 6 inches of rain in 4 hours, causing major landslides and flooding. At least a dozen people died and nearly 2,000 homes and businesses were destroyed.

**2001** – New York City: 19 terrorists hijacked 4 commercial airplanes loaded with passengers. Two of the hijacked airplanes intentionally flew into the World Trade Center buildings, causing them to collapse. At about the same time, a third airplane was intentionally crashed into the Pentagon building in Arlington, Virginia. A fourth aircraft crashed in a field near Shanksville Pennsylvania. It is believed the fourth plane was headed to the White House in Washington DC. 2,995 people were killed and more than 6,000 injured during these attacks. These events were a major turning point in American homeland security.

**1998 –** Central America: Hurricane Mitch, one of the most powerful hurricanes in history, killed nearly 11,000 people, causing massive damage.

**1997 –** Central Texas: Tornadoes caused 29 deaths, 32 injuries and an estimated $20 million in damage.

**1996 –** Northeast US: A massive blizzard dumped huge amounts of snow causing extensive problems. Resulting floods from melting snow caused more problems. An estimated 154 people died as a result of the blizzard, with more deaths resulting from the flooding. The storm caused over $3 billion in damage.

**1995 –** Oklahoma City, Oklahoma: The Alfred P. Murrah Federal building was destroyed when a truck filled with explosives detonated. 168 people were killed in the blast.

**1993** - New York City: A terrorist tried to blow up the World Trade Center but failed. Despite the failure to collapse the buildings, 6 people are killed and over 1,000 were injured.

**1992** - Hurricane Andrew (a category 5 storm) killed 26 people as it came ashore in south Florida and the Gulf Coast. Property damage was estimated at $25 billion. This was the most expensive natural disaster in U.S. history at the time.

**1991 –** Oakland, California: A wildfire killed 25 people and destroyed over 1,200 acres.

**1989 -** Loma Prieta California: An earthquake registering 6.9 on the Richter scale caused major damage in San Francisco and surrounding areas.

**1988 –** USA: An extended drought destroyed crops and fueled wildfires across the west. An estimated 5,000 – 10,000 people were believed to have died from heat related complications.

**1986 –** Ukraine: An explosion and fire in one of the Chernobyl nuclear reactors released radioactive material that spread over Russia and Europe. 31 people were said to have been killed and thousands more have had illnesses related to the incident.

**1985 -** Nevado Del Ruiz, Columbia: A volcano killed 25,000 people, most from a resulting mud flow.

**1985 –** Japan: A 747 airplane crashed into a mountain killing the 520 passengers and crew.

**1984 –** Bhopal, India: A pesticide plant released toxic gas into the atmosphere. The death toll varies, but it is believed to be between 2,000 and 16,000. A 2006 report stated there were over 558,000 people injured.

**1980 –** USA: A prolonged drought with excessive heat is believed to have killed over 10,000 people.

**1980 –** Mount St. Helens, Washington: A volcano erupted killing 57 people and destroyed more than 200 homes.

**1976 –** Tangshan, China: A magnitude 8 earthquake killed somewhere between 255,000 and 655,000 people.

**1975 –** Ru River, China: 230,000 people were killed when the Banqiao Dam collapsed. Massive flooding resulted.

**1970 –** Bangladesh: A hurricane and resulting floods killed between 500,000 – 1,000,000 people.

**1969** – Mississippi: Hurricane Camille, a Category 5 storm came ashore with winds in excess of 190 miles per hour.

**1966** – Austin, Texas: A gunman at the University of Texas went on a shooting rampage killing 16 and wounding 31 others.

**1962** – Tokyo, Japan: A freight train collided with a commuter train killing 163 and injuring 400.

**1953** – Waco, Texas: A tornado destroyed more than 850 homes and killed 114 people.

**1950** – Eastern US: A massive winter storm crippled the east coast. 353 people were believed to be killed as a result of the storm.

**1947**: Texas City, TX: A ship carrying munitions exploded in port causing a fire that destroyed much of the city. 516 people were killed.

**1940** – Midwest US: A blizzard killed 154 people as it took many by surprise with heavy snow and extreme cold.

**1933** – Long Beach, California: A 6.3 magnitude earthquake killed 115 people.

**1928** – Florida: A hurricane with 140+ mph winds killed more than 2,500 people as it came ashore.

**1927** – Bath, Michigan: An angry school board member blew up a school. 45 people were killed and 58 injured. Most of the victims were students.

**1925** – Illinois, Indiana & Missouri: A massive tornado destroyed homes and killed nearly 700 people as it tracked across the three states.

**1918** – An outbreak of Spanish Influenza killed over 500,000 people in the United States.

**1912** – North Atlantic Ocean: 1,517 passengers died when the Titanic sank after striking an iceberg. The Titanic was the largest passenger ship in the world at the time. It was thought to be unsinkable.

**1906** – San Francisco, California: An earthquake caused fires that burned for 4 days. More than 500 city blocks were destroyed, leaving 225,000 people homeless. An estimated 3,000 lives were lost.

**1904** – Eden, Colorado: A train derailed on a bridge during a flash flood. 96 people were killed.

**1902** – Mt. Pelee, West Indies: A volcanic eruption destroyed the city of St. Pierre and killed an estimated 40,000 people.

**1900** – Galveston, Texas: More than 8,000 were killed when a hurricane submerged the island.

**1889 /1890** – Russia: The Asiatic Flu killed more than 250,000 people in Europe alone. The disease also spread through South America, India and Australia with a high mortality rate.

**1889** – Johnstown, Pennsylvania: The town was flooded when the South Fork Dam burst. Over 2,200 were killed as 1,600 homes were washed away.

**1883** – Mt. Krakatoa, Indonesia: A volcano and subsequent tsunami killed more than 36,000 people.

**1881** – Vietnam: A hurricane killed an estimated 300,000 people.

**1881** – Chatsworth, Illinois: 81 people were killed and 372 injured when a burning trestle collapsed as a train passed over it.

**1871** – Illinois: A fire destroyed the business district of Chicago

**1871** – Wisconsin: A massive fire that occurred at the same time as the Great Chicago fire destroyed 12 towns and left nearly 1,200 people dead.

**1865** – Memphis, Tennessee: More than 1,500 people died when the Sultana, a river boat, sank in the Mississippi River after a boiler exploded on board.

**1840** – Natchez, Mississippi: 317 people were killed when a tornado struck. Death counts are believed to be higher because slaves were not counted.

**1816** – Mt. Tambora, India: An estimated 92,000 people were killed by a volcanic eruption and related causes.

**1811-12** – Missouri: Three of the strongest earthquakes in US history struck the southeast part of the state. Believed to have an estimated magnitude of 7.8 or higher, shaking was felt as far away as New York and Boston.

**1806** – Portsmouth New Hampshire: On Christmas Eve the city suffered a major fire.

**1802** – Portsmouth, New Hampshire: A Christmas day fire destroyed 132 buildings.

**1792** – Mt. Unzen, Japan – A volcanic eruption caused an avalanche that created a tsunami killing 12,000 – 15,000 people in nearby towns.

**1780** – Caribbean: A hurricane killed an estimated 20,000 as the storm hit the islands of Barbados and Martinique.

**1737** – India: An estimated 300,000 were killed when an earthquake induced typhoon struck Calcutta.

**1556** – China: An earthquake is believed to have killed 830,000 people.

**1348** – The Bubonic Plague, also known as the Black Death pandemic killed an estimated 75 million people, wiping out 30 to 60 percent of Europe's population.

**1287** – The Netherlands: 50,000 people were killed when a seawall on the Zuider Zee failed.

**1138** – Syria: A strong earthquake killed about 230,000 people. It is believed to be the fourth deadliest earthquake of all time.

**541** – Mediterranean region: A disease believed to be similar to the Bubonic Plague killed an estimated one quarter of the Byzantine population. The exact death toll is not known.

**526** – A massive earthquake struck the area currently known as Syria. The quake is believed to have killed 250,000 people.

**365** – An earthquake in the Mediterranean Sea destroyed nearly all the towns on the island of Crete. A resulting tsunami affected Alexandria Egypt and other nearby areas. Thousands of people are thought to have been killed.

**165 – 180** – Rome: Believed to be small pox or a measles pandemic, 5,000,000 people are believed to have died in what was known as the Antonine Plague, or the Plague of Galen.

**79** – Mt. Vesuvius, Italy: A volcano erupted destroying the towns of Pompeii and Herculaneum. More than 10,000 were killed.

**It could happen to you…**
**When the next disaster strikes, will you be ready?**

# Chapter 3

## Before the Disaster

The time to plan for what you'll do when disaster strikes is now. Don't wait until something happens to find you are not prepared. Understanding the concepts of emergency management will guide you through the basics of the planning process.

Emergency management is based on the four basic principles: Mitigation, Preparedness, Response and Recovery. Although the four phases of emergency management are four distinct categories, they are a continuous circle. After the recovery phase, the mitigation phase starts again. Each phase compliments the next. The planning circle can begin at any phase. The 4 phases are applicable to any disaster and can be adapted to situation.

Patrol level officers rarely are involved in the logistics of upper level emergency management and planning, but it is still good to at least have a working knowledge of what happens behind the scenes. You can adapt the concepts to your own personal scenarios to improve the outcome of disasters.

### Mitigation

This is the act of making an effort to reduce the impact of hazards. Simply put, it is preventing problems before they happen. For government agencies, mitigation is accomplished through the use of building codes and construction procedures. Actions such as building a stronger home to withstand an earthquake, or building structures high above flood zones can minimize problems if a disaster strikes. Mitigation reduces the probability of physical damage or injury resulting from a potential disaster.

**Preparedness**

This is the act of people actually preparing for a hazard. Preparedness ensures you will be ready to respond to and handle a disaster. Making sure you have an emergency kit, having adequate supplies and knowing what to do if emergency services are not available are all acts of preparedness. This practices the idea of being *proactive* rather than *reactive*. Training falls into this category.

**Response**

These are the actions taken to respond to an actual emergency or disaster. Response would include fire fighters responding to fires, medical personnel treating the injured and police securing danger areas. Knowing what to expect during a disaster will make for a more efficient and a more effective response. This translates to lives being saved.

**Recovery**

The goal of recovery is to return your life and community back to the pre-disaster condition. Restoring essential services, fixing roads and bridges and rebuilding homes and lives occur in this phase.

In most jurisdictions, emergency management is handling by an Emergency Manager. Emergency Managers can work for cities, counties and state agencies. An Emergency Manager is the person responsible for coordinating resources during an event. The Emergency Manager can be called in at any time during the disaster response. This person must ensure that all critical needs are covered to provide continuity of critical services and the protection of life and property in their jurisdictional area. The Emergency Manager will act as a central point of communication for everyone involved in the response. This involves extensive planning before an event and communication and teamwork during an incident.

The Emergency Manager works closely with any potential responding agencies. This includes police, fire, ems, public works, volunteer groups, private businesses, the military and others. Everyone involved must share in the planning. Everyone needs to be on the same page and must understand their roles.

**Creating an Emergency Plan**

The first thing to do before a disaster is to learn what types of threats you could potentially be exposed to. This is called a hazard analysis. The purpose of a hazard analysis is to assess your risks and identify ways of controlling or eliminating them. By doing this, you can focus on hazards that are more likely to occur than others. For example, if you live in Minnesota, your chance of being impacted by a hurricane is far less than if you live in Florida. Or, your chance of encountering a blizzard is less in south Texas, than in Maine. It's not to say that the event could not occur, but it is less probable. You can learn more about specific threats in your area by contacting your local emergency management office.

We all hope we will never have to encounter a disaster. The truth is you may have to so it is very important to have a plan. It is critical for agencies to have plans in place, but you also need to think about yourself and your family. Each individual person should develop a plan and every family should have a plan. Planning brings out many questions that you must address. Creating a personalized emergency plan will help you deal with a disaster in a less stressful manner.

What will you do if a disaster occurs? Where will you or others go if there is an evacuation? What if you can't get to your kids or spouse?    Will *they* know what to do? Think of ways to lessen the effects of disaster in your own life as well as at work. After you create your plan, be sure to share it with your family. Practice your plans regularly and make sure *everyone* involved understands them fully. The following information can be a great resource for your family, but it is also valuable information to share with citizens of your community.

## Important Tips for the Home

Everyone should develop an escape plan for homes and businesses in case you need to get out quickly during an emergency. Plan an emergency exit in each room of your home. Always have a back-up exit plan as your primary exit may be blocked. Remember, disasters may occur while you are away from home. Always plan escape routes in hotels or other buildings you may be in. If in a high rise building, use a stairway. Do not use elevators to escape. Designate a meeting point outside the home or business. You should also have a second, back up meeting spot somewhere away from your home. Designate a spot to meet and be sure everyone with you knows where to go.

Every home should have a fire extinguisher. Most people keep an extinguisher in the kitchen, but it's also a good idea to have one in the bedroom, the garage and in your car. Know where your fire extinguisher is and be sure everyone else knows. Make sure everyone knows how to use it. Many fire departments offer "live fire" training on the proper use of extinguishers. Read the instructions prior to use to understand how they should be used, as there are various types of fires. The most common and best extinguisher to have is an "A,B,C" type (5lb). This is a multi-purpose extinguisher that can be used on a variety of fires.

Extinguishers should only be used on small fires. In the case of a large fire, summon fire rescue assistance if possible. In the case of a structure fire, get everyone out immediately. Always inform the public to call 911 from outside the home. Once outside, do not go back inside the fire area to retrieve belongings.

Become familiar with home utilities and know how to shut them off. If you need to evacuate your home, it is best shut off your utilities before leaving. You should know how to use the water valve, electrical box and gas shut off. If gas is turned off, it should only be turned back on by a trained professional. If you are not sure how to use your utilities, seek assistance. Many of these tactics are utilized by CERT teams in a disaster. If you can learn to do these things and if you can teach your family, it will aid responders in a major disaster.

**Schools**

Talk with schools in your jurisdiction to find out what type of disaster plans they have in place. Ask if your local school keeps a supply of food, water, and other emergency supplies. Does your school practice emergency drills for a variety of disaster scenarios? Find out if school employees are trained on emergency response procedures. If they are not, encourage them to seek training.

If a school must shelter in place, parents may not be permitted to pick up their children. The doors will most likely be locked during an incident as a precaution to keep the children safe. This can often cause panic with parents. It may also cause traffic and crowd control problems. Be aware of school procedures.

Find out how your local school communicates with families during emergency situations. Make sure your school has current emergency parent contact information on file. Always encourage them to have backup contacts in case someone is not available.

Get involved during school drills to ensure understanding of policies and procedures. If you have questions or suggestions about emergency planning, feel free to contact administrators. They should be willing to address your concerns.

**Work**

Every workplace should have plans in place for an emergency. Every building should have an evacuation plan. All employees should be aware of the plan and everyone should participate in emergency drills. Think about what would happen if you were not allowed to leave work. Would you have adequate supplies? Does your workplace have an emergency supply kit? This will be discussed in depth in later chapters, but imagine if you were stuck in your station for one, two or even three days. It's important to get businesses involved in the emergency planning process.

Business owners and managers should learn about emergency planning processes in order to ensure the safety of employees in the workplace. All of the planning tips in this book can be applied to homes or businesses. Businesses should appoint a safety representative to assist with the emergency planning process. Business owners have the responsibility of creating a safe workplace for employees and customers.

Public safety agencies are no different. Take into account the needs of office staff and dispatchers. Dispatch employees may not be able to leave for extended periods in the event of major incident. What types of plans do you have in place for them? Having office staff and other critical employees presents challenges that are often overlooked. Administrators must take the needs of these employees into account.

## Business Continuity

Many agencies fail to properly plan for disasters. A major event could cause serious disruptions for organizations that are not prepared. Whether you operate a small one man department, or a large metropolitan agency, the plans should be the same. Buildings could become damaged and rendered unusable. Critical equipment may be lost or damaged. Employees may not be able to make it in to work because of illness or hazard related issues. Evaluate your risks and take precautions before a disaster strikes.

If your agency plans to operate during and after a disaster, it is important to have a contingency plan in place. Do you have back up power sources if the public utilities go down? If your agency utilizes equipment that relies on electricity, be sure to have an appropriate power generator and fuel to support operations. If your primary business location is not able to be used, plan for an alternate operating location ahead of time.

The most important thing for agencies to consider is having a backup for critical systems and documents.

Do not store all of your important files in one location. Have copies of important documents and store them in a secure location.

Things such as payroll, records, inventory and other operational documents should be stored on portable hard drives, internet based storage or at satellite locations. If you need to evacuate or close your station, you can bring the portable storage with you.

This is important not just for administrators, but also patrol officers. Consider what you use on a day to day basis. Try to simplify what you use and think about how you would get along without it.

If employees are not able to make it to work, could your agency continue to operate? Staffing can become a major issue during times of disease pandemic. Staff may not be able to make it to work due to roads being closed or inaccessible. You may be forced to work with limited staffing. Employees should be cross trained prior to a disaster. Be sure everyone understands what may be expected of them should a superior be unable to fulfill the necessary duties of the job. This is important whether you are a patrol officer, or the chief.

Having knowledge of the duties of other employees can make things run smoother. If employees know how to handle other positions, your business can continue to operate with minimum staffing. Managers can also consider having employees work from home if it is appropriate for your business. Sickness is a major cause of lost revenue.

Contagious disease can cripple even the largest of operations. Businesses should limit the exposure of sick employees. Sick employees should stay home if possible. Encourage the use of hand sanitizers and hand washing to limit the spread of germs in the workplace.

## Communication

It is important to let your staff and the public know the status of your community. If you have a website, information can be published online. For employees, create a phone list or phone tree. Maintain contacts with media outlets such as television stations, radio or newspapers. Appoint a public information officer to inform everyone what the status of your agency is.

## Other Planning Considerations

Become familiar with threats and warnings. Discuss with your employees and families what they should do if alerted. Discuss with your family what they would do if you were not at home when a disaster happens. Also discuss different threats and warnings with your children. Be sure to practice emergency drills with your family. This can ease fear and make the situation less stressful during an actual event. Be sure to act when an alert is made.

Keep recent photos of your family members and pets. You can provide a photo to authorities if anyone should become lost in a disaster.

Become certified in basic first aid and CPR. Encourage your family and co-workers to become certified. These trainings are offered by the American Red Cross and American Heart Association as well as other organizations. Official certification by the American Red Cross provides legal protection for those giving first aid under the "Good Samaritan" law. The courses are low cost and can save lives.

Always wear a medical alert bracelet if you have special health concerns. Persons with special needs such as the disabled or elderly should prepare with extra care.

If you know of anyone with special needs, be sure that you know where they are during an incident. Be sure to check on them in an emergency as they may not see or hear warnings.

Allow extra time in dealing with their needs. Disabilities may hinder evacuation or rescue as some people may not have received warnings or information due to disabilities. Research the needs of those with special issues in your jurisdiction. This is a great community policing project for those who want to get more involved.

Many public safety agencies keep registers of people with disabilities. This aids in locating those with disabilities during a disaster or emergency response. Contact your local fire department or emergency management office for more information.

Encourage your agency to put on a "safety fair" or a similar public event. This is a great opportunity for multiple agencies to promote preparedness and safety tips. It allows everyone, young and old to get involved. Talk to families about response capabilities and resources. Teach children how and when to use 911 to summon emergency services. Hold a CPR or First Aid class.

Other methods of public education include cooperation with insurance agents. It is important to understand what insurance policies cover and what they don't. Consider purchasing or updating insurance for your own home and belongings before a disaster strikes. If you rent or lease your home or an apartment, consider renters insurance. Insurance agents are usually more than happy to assist with spreading the word about safety.

Any often overlooked type of protection is flood insurance. This is critical if you live in flood prone areas, but it is not usually included as a part of standard insurance policies. Consult an insurance agent for more information regarding these policies.

We plan and prepare so we can minimize the risk of property damage, injury or death. Don't wait until something happens to find out you are not prepared. Take some time to think your individual needs and the needs of your family. Get involved with the community. If the public is better prepared, it will make the response better for all involved.

# CHAPTER 4

## When Disaster Strikes

If there is an impending event you will be notified by authorities. The most common alert notification is the Emergency Alert System. This is the warning tones heard on TV and radio stations which are followed by instructions. You may also be alerted by warning sirens, weather radios, or by telephone. If time permits, newspapers or magazines may also provide warning information. These warnings will inform you as to whether you should stay where you are, or go somewhere else for safety. You should be sure to follow the instructions provided by authorities to ensure your safety.

When a disaster occurs, the first responders to the scene will be local police, fire and emergency medical providers. If you live in a large city, you will have many resources at your disposal. However, if you live in a rural area or small town, services are often limited. Responders will have many duties to attend to, as initial resources will be limited and back up may be delayed.

During even a small scale event, first response resources can easily be overwhelmed. Even large cities can become overwhelmed quickly. Equipment may be damaged or responders may be injured. There simply aren't enough responders to help during a major incident. This is part of why we must learn to maximize our effectiveness.

### Disaster Operations:

Cities both large and small must rely on what is called a mutual aid agreement. This is a plan that is arranged long before a disaster strikes.

It allows public safety agencies to rely on other surrounding agencies to provide extra assistance when needed. Hospitals must also have a similar plan in place. Imagine a rural hospital with only a few beds having to handle a mass casualty event. They simply could not handle the overload of patients. Where would the incoming casualties go? What if other nearby hospitals were closed? Cities and organizations, like individuals, need to always have a backup plan.

When local resources are overwhelmed, the next level of assistance will come from the state. State resources may include state law enforcement or fire agencies. These resources may be delayed do the unforeseen conditions in an emergency, or they may be coming from a far distance. If an emergency is serious enough, the Governor of the state can also activate National Guard units to respond for assistance. If state agencies become overwhelmed the Governor can also request help from other states. If the disaster extends beyond the response of available state resources, the Governor can declare a state of emergency which will then start the process of assistance from the federal government.

**Federal Response**

Federal resources cannot get involved until after local and state resources have been overwhelmed and the Governor has declared a state of emergency. After a state Governor has declared a state of emergency, the President can then authorize federal response assistance and resources to be directed to the disaster area. Federal assistance includes the resources of the Federal Emergency Management Agency. Assistance may come in the form of additional emergency responders, supplies or financial aid for agencies involved in the response. Federal resources may also provide financial assistance to help with the recovery effort after the event is over. Federal resources may take up to 3 days to arrive at the disaster site. This is why you need to be prepared to sustain yourself. Having adequate emergency supplies will allow you to sustain yourself during this period if help is not immediately available.

Private organizations such as the Red Cross or faith based groups may assist at any time during the response, but only at the direction of emergency management officials.

Volunteers can be an excellent resource during disasters, but only if managed properly. If you wish to volunteer during a disaster, you should receive training before an incident occurs. Untrained and unsolicited volunteers may be turned away from a disaster scene as they may present more of a hazard than help. Check with local service organizations to find out about training for disaster response. Many agencies have programs such as Senior Patrols, Explorers, Community Services Officers and Animal Control. All of these programs can be utilized in your response.

In a large event, an emergency operations center (EOC) may need to be opened. The emergency operations center is a safe, secure location that provides logistical support and coordination for responders. The primary function of the EOC is to collect, gather and analyze data to assist the decision making process. With the hectic environment of disaster multi-tasking, someone needs to coordinate the response. The person in charge of the EOC is the city, county or regional Emergency Manager (EM). EOC's can also be activated for other high profile scenarios such as concerts, sporting events, political events, and anything else that may require extensive resources. The EOC is used for support, but not to manage the incident.

Tactical management decisions are carried out from an incident command post. An incident command post is usually set up at a location near the disaster, but out of immediate danger. The EOC and incident command post must communicate to relay important information to each other about the incident. The incident command post is managed by an Incident Commander.

The first person on scene at an incident is usually considered the Incident Commander (IC) until he or she relieves the duties to someone more qualified. The IC duties can be assumed by patrol level supervisors or administration. The IC has full authority over the incident, so the person must be capable of handling the duties.

If an incident requires it, the IC can appoint personnel to carry specific functions such as safety, public information and liaison services. This is what is referred to as the Incident Command System. The Incident Command System is flexible in that it can grow or shrink to meet incident management needs. It provides the much needed control that disasters or large events can present when dealing with multiple agencies and resources.

## Incident Command System

Incident management and staffing can be a difficult task. A system needs to be implemented to assist with the leadership operations of emergency response. The Incident Command System (ICS) is useful tool adopted by many agencies to assist with the operation and control of an incident. It allows personnel from different agencies and jurisdictions to work together as one. It allows for an integrated organizational structure that provides a more efficient method of managing events, large or small, regardless of the incident type. ICS also allows responders to communicate more efficiently by using common terminology, rather than radio codes which may vary by agency. As a responder, you will most likely be working under an ICS system in the event of a large incident or multi-agency response.

In the old days of emergency management, responders were often hindered by poor communication, lack of planning, overloaded incident commanders and no requirements for integration between agencies. ICS was created as a way to solve these issues. To resolve jurisdictional conflicts and confusion, ICS allows the most qualified person to oversee operations, rather than the highest ranking. This allows for better management decisions.

## The 5 Functions of ICS

In a traditional ICS system, there are 5 main functions. These functions can be increased or decreased as the needs of the incident require.

**Command**: Sets objectives and priorities at incident and has overall command.

**Operations**: Conducts tactical operations to carry out plans. Develops tactical objectives and organization, and directs all tactical resources.

**Planning**: Prepares and documents the Incident Action Plan to accomplish objectives, collects and evaluates information, maintains resource status, and maintains documentation for incident records.

**Logistics**: Provides support, resources and other services needed to support incident needs.

**Finance / Administration**: Monitors costs related to the incident. Also provides accounting, procurement, time recording and cost analyses.

Responders may also work under what is known as Unity of Command. This means all individual responders work under only one supervisor. It also allows for better tracking of resources. Effective management creates a more effective response.

During and after a disaster there will certainly be chaos, confusion and fear. Roads may be closed or inaccessible as a result of damage or debris. Transportation facilities and hospitals may be shut down, damaged or destroyed. Communications will most likely be affected. During the event, you may be stranded where you are. A perfect example of this was during Hurricane Katrina in 2005. Residents and visitors who did not evacuate were stranded when roads in and out of the city were cut off. During the terrorist attacks of September 11th 2001, every airport in the United States was closed. Every airplane in the sky was forced to land where ever they were. Many travelers were stranded in cities far from home for an extended period of time. With so many people stranded, telephone lines were overwhelmed by hundreds of thousands of callers trying to communicate with friends and family.

With roads and highways closed or inaccessible, you may not be able to make it back to your home or you may not be able to leave home if you are sheltered in place. At the same time, rescuers may not be able to get to respond in a timely manner. Responders may not have the ability to get to the people that need rescue. This is why it is very important to encourage the public to have a plan and an emergency kit at home and work, as well as in vehicles.

## Response Hazards

When responding to a disaster, extra care must be used. Take a breath and calm down. Think before you respond. Maintain a view of the roadway well ahead of your vehicle. Drive at a reasonable and prudent speed. Be sure to take into account special conditions such as ice, snow, flooding, fog or smoke. Visibility may be limited, traffic may be congested or there may be hazards in the roadway.

Watch for downed power lines. You may not be able to immediately tell if a power line is "hot" or not. Do not drive over power lines. Beware of downed trees or poles that may be in the roadway. Also watch for other road debris such as metal, rocks or anything else that could cause damage to your vehicle. If you are driving into a threat area, be prepared for what you going into.

Upon arrival, you should follow your agency policies and procedures. As mentioned in the ICS section, if you are the first responding unit, you are in charge until properly relieved. This means it is your duty to inform other responders about any potential threats or needs. You will be the one calling the shots. If there is a need for additional police units, fire apparatus or rescue equipment, request them immediately. Direct the resources to where they need to go.

If your initial response does not have adequate resources, don't try to be a hero. You are no good to the rescue if you are hurt or killed. We should serve as the rescuers, not the rescued.

The primary role of all first responders is saving lives. Police officers in a disaster response need to contain the situation. To make for an efficient response, officers should try to establish a perimeter to secure the scene as soon as possible. Unnecessary personnel and citizens should not be allowed in the area of the incident. Different safety zones extending from the center point of the incident should be established. Be sure to consider things such as wind direction, threat location and the chance of additional threats when deciding on a perimeter. It is always better to start with a large perimeter. It can always be scaled down later if needed.

When dealing with explosions, train derailments, hazardous materials or industrial accidents, the incident should be treated as a crime scene until it is known otherwise. Incidents could be an act of terrorism.

Crowd control must be managed to maintain safety of the involved responders and assisting in the rescue of the injured. It is your job to protect those who are making rescues. Traffic control is essential to create a safe route for responders coming and going. Roads should be blocked off, allowing only emergency responders and other necessary equipment into the disaster area.

Officers should also aid in the rescue of the injured if staffing permits.

**Aiding the Injured**

Ensure that you are in a safe position before attempting first aid so you will not cause further injury. Be aware of hazards such as debris, wires, fire or structural damage. If a serious injury has occurred, seek appropriate medical attention immediately. You should only attempt to provide first aid for the skills and knowledge you have been trained on. This book is not meant to serve as a first aid training guide. You should attend an in-person training course to improve your first aid knowledge and skills.

## Triage

When rescuers arrive at the scene of a disaster or mass casualty incident, they must do what is known as triage.

Triage is the quick assessment of injuries to determine who is in the most immediate need of help. Triage is also routinely used in hospitals and walk in care clinics.

Triage is based on a color coded tag system. When a rescuer checks patients in a mass casualty incident, they are assigned a tag. In civilian response, the four colors typically used are green, yellow, red and black. The US Military uses a slightly different system, based on the same concept. Each color represents the level of emergency care needed. Patients with the most serious injuries will be treated first. Those with minor injuries can wait to seek medical attention.

### Triage Color Codes

**Black**: Used for those who are deceased, or who will most likely not survive, even with rapid emergency care.

**Red**: Used for those with serious life threatening injuries. These patients may not survive without immediate emergency care.

**Yellow**: Used for patients with more serious, but non-life threatening injuries. These patients can wait for treatment.

**Green**: Used for patients with minor injuries. These patients do not require immediate emergency care or treatment.

Medical facilities and rescuers will be overwhelmed in a major incident. If you are not seriously injured, let rescuers tend to those who are. With basic first aid skills, you may be able to help yourself. This will allow rescuers to handle an incident more efficiently.

## Basic First Aid

Note: In order to avoid possible health contamination risks, always use latex or rubber gloves. It is always best to attend a first aid course so you can learn the proper techniques to help yourself and others in emergency situations.

## First: Check for any obvious injuries.

## Unconscious / Not Breathing

Do not attempt to move a seriously injured or unconscious person unless they are in immediate danger of death or further serious injury. If you must move an injured or unconscious person, first stabilize the neck and back, then call for help immediately if you can.

Shake the person and ask "are you okay" to see if you can get a response. If there is no response, remain calm and do a patient assessment.

## If you find an unconscious person, remember your "ABC"s (Airway / Breathing / Circulation):

**A**: Be sure to check the **airway** for any obstructions. If there are any foreign objects, clear them with a finger sweep.

**B**: Place one hand on the victim's forehead. Carefully raise the chin back. Is the person **breathing**? Place your ear next to the victim's mouth and listen for breath sounds. Look for any rise or movement in the chest.

**C**: Does the person have **circulation** (a pulse)?

If the person is not breathing or does not have a pulse, carefully position the victim to administer CPR (Cardiopulmonary Resuscitation).

Procedures for CPR change periodically. You should attend a CPR training course to ensure your knowledge of the most current CPR techniques. If you have access to an Automatic External Defibrillator (AED), this is a great life-saving tool. An AED is a device used to restart the heart. Many CPR courses will also instruct you on the use of these devices.

**Bleeding**: Attempt to control bleeding through the use of direct pressure. Apply constant pressure on the wound using a towel or dressing. Use sterile dressings if possible. Untreated bleeding can lead to shock. Proper wound management and cleaning is best done by professional medical staff. If the bleeding gets worse or cannot be controlled, seek professional help as soon as possible.

**Broken Bones**: Do not try to straighten an extremity if it is deformed or if bones are protruding. If there is any bleeding, try to control it. Keep the injury in the position where it is and try to stabilize it. If medical assistance is not readily available, use padding or a splint to keep it from moving. If you are able to elevate the injured extremity without causing further injury, do so to prevent swelling.

Put ice on the injury, but not directly on the skin (place the ice in a plastic bag or towel). Keep the ice on the injury for 20 minutes, then take it off for 20 minutes, then repeat. Over the counter pain killers can help to ease the pain.

If the person feels faint or if breathing is short or rapid, lay the person down with the head slightly lower than the trunk and, if possible, elevate the legs.

**Burns**: Minor burns (slightly reddened skin with no blisters) can be treated with a topical burn ointment or spray. Use water to cool the burn. Over the counter pain killers can be used to ease the pain of minor burns. If there is charring, blistering or if skin is peeling, these are indicators of a serious injury and complications are likely. Seek professional medical attention as soon as possible. Any burns to the face, hands, feet or genital area should also be treated by a professional.

Do not apply butter or oils to burns. Cover the wound with sterile dressings. Wear loose fitting clothing while burns are healing.

**Shock**: Shock can be a serious, life threatening medical condition. Shock is caused by decreased blood flow to the brain and other extremities. Look for signs of altered mental state, empty stare in the eyes, rapid shallow breathing and cool, clammy skin. Ensure the injured person has a clear airway. Reassure the person and have them lie down with the feet elevated. Prevent the loss the body heat with a blanket. Be sure the victim does not become overheated.

Do not attempt to give an unconscious person anything by mouth. If there is bleeding, it needs to be controlled. If there is vomiting, roll the victim to one side and sweep the vomit from his or her mouth with your fingers. Continue to check on the victim until medical assistance can be obtained.

## Searches

If it is safe to go outside, walk around the exterior of buildings to check for structural damage. If a building has suffered any flood, fire or storm damage, stay out. If you have any doubts about the stability of a structure, do not re-enter it until it has been inspected by a professional. If authorities have declared a home or building to be unsafe, stay out of it. Debris or potentially contaminated materials may also be present.

If it is possible to check a building, a thorough search must be conducted to check for victims. This should be done the as a search during an alarm or when trying to locate a suspect. You must tactically move through the home. Beware of threats inside the home. Residents may be in shock or confused. They may not know who you are, especially if it is dark. Be sure to identify yourself before entering.

Know that some people may not be happy to see you. Extremists or criminals may not want the police checking their homes. They may be armed and could have ambushes or booby traps set up. Use caution when searching and never search alone.

Be sure to keep track of what has been searched so responders do not waste time re-checking property. Document locations searched. A simple reference to mark buildings that have been checked is to leave an ID on the home. When entering a structure, make a slash mark ( / ). When exiting the structure, make another opposite slash ( X ). A n X lets others responders know the area has been checked. If there is only a half slash ( / ), responders can know someone is inside the structure searching.

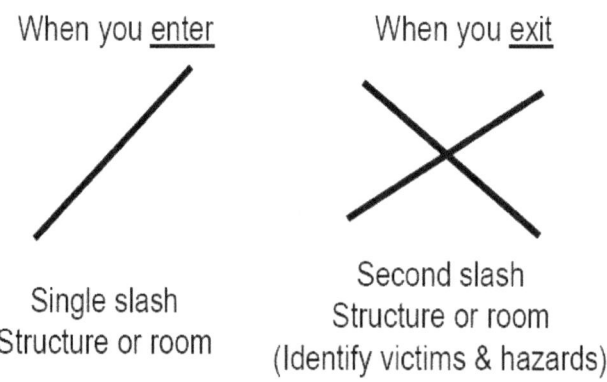

When you <u>enter</u>

When you <u>exit</u>

Single slash
Structure or room

Second slash
Structure or room
(Identify victims & hazards)

It is also good to list the date and time the building was checked. You should also list any hazards or victims found as well as who checked the structure (agency, task force, etc.).

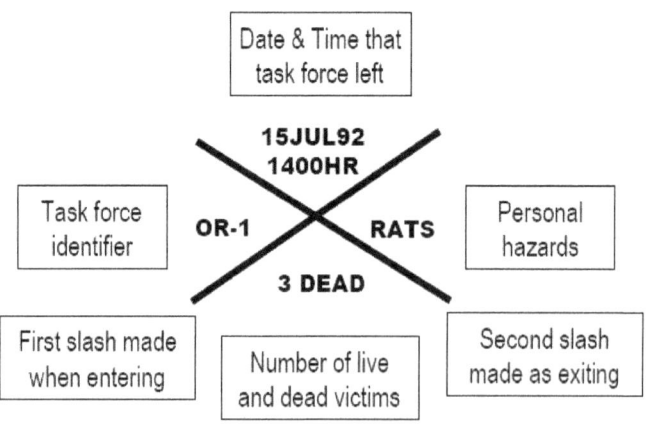

Date & Time that
task force left

15JUL92
1400HR

Task force
identifier

OR-1

RATS

Personal
hazards

First slash made
when entering

Number of live
and dead victims

Second slash
made as exiting

3 DEAD

(Images courtesy of FEMA)

46

## Safety Issues

Be aware of new safety issues created by the disaster. Watch for contaminated water, broken glass, damaged electrical wiring, and slippery floors. Watch out for animals, especially poisonous snakes. Wear a helmet, long pants, boots and gloves. Use a stick to poke through debris. Be aware of an increase in insects as well. If handling debris, wear safety glasses also.

If communications permit, advise your local authorities about any health and safety issues. Chemical spills, downed power lines, washed out roads, and dead animals are concerns that should be promptly addressed.

## Hazardous Materials

Hazardous materials are around us every day. Chemicals are used in many aspects of industrial production. They help to improve our lives but they can also cause havoc if they are used improperly or released accidentally. Responders need to be aware of the potential threats of these materials.

Some of the most dangerous chemicals in the world pass through our cities and neighborhoods every day. Trains and trucks passing by our homes, schools, churches, and businesses have the potential to cause major problems because of the hazardous cargo they carry. These materials can come in the form of explosives, flammable and combustible substances, poisons, and radioactive materials.

Occasionally accidents can occur during industrial production, storage, transportation, use, or disposal of these materials. Your community could be at risk if a chemical is used or stored in an unsafe manner. Chemicals are sometimes released in harmful amounts into the environment where you live, work, or play. The release may be an accident, or it may be intentional, as hazardous materials are also a point of interest with terrorists. Buildings or vehicles that store hazardous materials could be damaged or destroyed in a disaster scenario.

If there is a release of hazardous chemicals, try to stay away from the source. If you are outside, get as far away as possible from the danger area. Try to stay upstream, uphill, and upwind from the threat. Tell others to move out of the area. Avoid inhaling any gases, fumes and smoke. Cover your mouth with a cloth while evacuating the area.

If you witness or respond to an accident involving a tanker truck or train, do not approach the vehicle. If you see any spilled liquids, airborne mists, or condensed solid chemical deposits, get as far away as possible, and do not touch or smell them.

Notify the appropriate responding authorities of what you see. If you see any victims in the danger area, do not approach or touch them until the hazardous material has been identified. Do not enter contaminated areas without wearing proper personal protective equipment.

If there is a hazardous material release, quickly advise nearby people to get inside. Tell them to close and lock all exterior doors and windows. Close all vents, fireplace dampers, and as many interior doors as possible. Turn off air conditioners and ventilation systems. In large buildings, ventilation systems should be set to 100 percent recirculation so no outside air is drawn into the building. If this is not possible, ventilation systems should be turned off completely.

When entering buildings, there may be damage. If there is potential of hazardous materials being in a damaged building, do not enter it. Look for warning signs that may indicate a potential threat. A great resource to have is the Emergency Response Guidebook. This is a guidebook for use by first responders during the initial phases of a hazardous materials incident. It covers information about specific chemicals and the threats they pose. It informs responders of what procedures should be followed and what personal protective equipment is required. The book is available through the US Department of Transportation. Best of all, it's free for all public safety agencies.

**Gas Leaks**

If a home or business utilizes natural gas service, leaks are a major hazard. If you hear a hissing or roaring sound around gas meters or appliances, there may have a leak. Other signs of a leak include appliances failing to ignite, bubbling puddles of water in the yard or around gas meters and dead vegetation around gas meters. If you detect the pungent odor of rotten eggs, this is an additive in natural gas to let you know of a leak. If you notice any of these indicators, leave the area immediately and notify dispatch or your local gas service authority. Do not turn on light switches or use your phone in the area of a possible leak and do not use lighters, matches or any other open flame.

**Personal Health**

Be aware of exhaustion. Don't try to do too much at once. Set priorities and pace yourself. Get enough rest, eat well and drink plenty of clean water. Wash your hands thoroughly with soap and water often when working in or around debris. Pay attention to the environmental conditions and dress accordingly.

**Evacuation**

Before, or during a disaster, citizens may need to be evacuated for their safety. Evacuations are more common than most people think. Evacuations occur hundreds of times each year due to storms, fires, industrial accidents or hazardous chemical spills. You may have advance warning to evacuate in some situations. Some events such as hurricanes can allow you advance notice of a day or two. Other fast acting situations will not give any warning. You may need to leave with only a moment notice.

You will alerted by your local emergency manager as to what you should do and where people should go. The decision to evacuate will be based on the perceived threat. Your individual situation may vary depending on your location, your shelter and the intensity of the pending incident.

Residents may be required to go to a shelter for protection. Shelters are often located in places such as school gymnasiums, churches or other buildings able to accommodate large groups of people with protection from the threat. Be sure to follow all instructions provided to minimize risk of injury or property damage.

*If time and staffing permit, check for contraband or hazardous items on people who are entering shelters.*

If citizens are evacuating on their own, it is critical to provide information about following instructions for the recommended safest route out of the affected area. Ensure these routes are well managed and kept clear for those leaving. It is common for people to want to head into the disaster area to get to loved ones or to provide help. This may be dangerous and could potentially cause more problems. Prevent citizens from entering or returning to the disaster area if possible. Residents can only return home after being told it is safe to do so. Tell citizens to stay tuned to a radio or television for information on evacuation routes, temporary shelters, and procedures.

## Animals / Pets

Don't forget to plan ahead for the care of pets. Pets are often considered to be members of the family. Citizens should always have an emergency plan in place to ensure the safety and care of pets in the event of a disaster. Pets may not be able to go with their owners to evacuation centers. With the exception of service animals, most pets are not typically permitted in emergency shelters as they may affect the health and safety of humans. Check with pet boarding facilities to find out what, if any disaster plans they have in place. Encourage the public to seek out information before a disaster.

Citizens with large farm animals such as horses, cattle, sheep, goats, or pigs should also develop an emergency plan before a disaster. Animals should all have some form of identification in case they get loose. Encourage animal owners to secure their property before evacuating. Wandering animals could pose a safety or health hazard.

## Shelter in Place

Homes and businesses should have a pre-selected shelter room. This room should be above ground and should have the fewest openings to the outside (Chemicals in the air will sink, so you will be safer in a higher location).

In case of an airborne chemical or radiological threat, gaps under doorways and windows should be sealed with wet towels or plastic sheeting and duct tape. You will also want to seal any gaps around air conditioning units, bathroom and kitchen exhaust fans, and any stove or dryer vents with duct tape and plastic sheeting, wax paper or aluminum wrap. This may help to prevent contaminated air from entering the home. Use additional material to fill any cracks or holes in the room.

People often have concerns about sealing themselves in the home. This is a valid point as there are always hazardous chemicals in every home. Houses are made to ventilate. This prevents the buildup of carbon dioxide. Ten square feet of floor space per person will provide sufficient air to prevent carbon dioxide build up for up to five hours, assuming normal breathing rates while resting. However, it is not recommended that you shelter yourself in a sealed room for more than 2-3 hours. Sheltering in place is only a short term solution.

The effectiveness of such sheltering diminishes with time as the carbon dioxide levels build. Contaminated air outside can also gradually seep in, as it not possible to seal every leak in your home. Evacuation from the area is recommended if a prolonged toxic event is expected.

If you are exposed to gas or vapors that have entered your shelter, take shallow breaths through a cloth or a towel held over your mouth and nose. Avoid eating or drinking anything that may be contaminated.

Some people choose to have breathing respirators or gas masks in their emergency supply kit. These are available at military surplus stores or other businesses that sell survival supplies.

If you have been exposed to any chemicals, seek medical assistance immediately. If information is available from authorities, follow decontamination instructions. You may be advised to take a thorough shower, or you may be advised to stay away from water and follow another decontamination method.

Clothing may need to be disposed of. Be sure to place the contaminated items in a tightly sealed container. Do not let the contaminated items come into contact with other items or people. If you come into contact with other people, tell them you may have been contaminated with a toxic substance. Avoid physical contact until you have been properly decontaminated.

In the event of an incident, citizens may initially be asked to shelter in place, but needs may arise that require an evacuation. If told to evacuate, it is extremely important that this is accomplished immediately and in an orderly fashion. Decontamination centers may need to be set up. Residents will need to be directed to these locations if required.

If there is time before leaving, contamination can be minimized in homes by closing all windows, shutting all air vents, and turning off attic fans.

After the event is over, homes and businesses should be thoroughly ventilated to remove any residual contamination. Ask local hazardous material handlers how to properly clean your home or property.

Report any remaining hazards to appropriate emergency services personnel.

**If hazardous waste is present, it should only be removed by trained professionals.**

**Check with your local emergency management office to find out what types of hazardous material threats are in your area.**

# CHAPTER 5

## Emergency Supplies

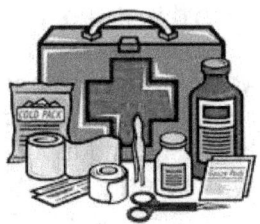

If a disaster should occur, you may not have access to grocery stores or other needs. Businesses may be closed or damaged. Roads may not be passable. You may be stranded at home or another location for an extended period of time. It is because of this that we must be prepared to sustain ourselves for an extended period of time. Your emergency kit should contain water, food, first aid supplies and other items that will allow you and your family to be self-sufficient for at least 3 days.

Prior to an anticipated event there is often a rush to purchase emergency supplies. Supplies may be limited, or gone at the time a disaster is upon you. If you plan ahead you can have peace of mind knowing you are prepared. The following are items you should have on hand *before* a disaster occurs.

### Water

You should plan on having a minimum of one gallon of water per person, per day. You should store at least a 3 day supply of water. Water for drinking should be stored in clean containers that can be tightly sealed. If you do not have your own containers, simply purchase bottled water at your local grocery store. Your stored water supply should be kept in a cool dark place. Do not leave water exposed to direct sunlight. Rotate your drinking water supply at least every 6 months.

Don't forget that water will also be needed for pets, brushing your teeth, bathing, washing food, dishes or for general cleaning.

People who live in hot climates, children, pets, sick people and nursing mothers often require more water. If you are active or working in the elements you should have extra water stored.

Never ration water unless told to do so. Stocking up on water before a disaster is the best thing to do, but if you are caught off guard, there are many water sources in and around your home that can be used during an emergency. Some of the sources below may not be safe to drink without purification. Information on purifying water can be found later in this chapter. Utilizing these emergency resources would be a "worst case" scenario if no other water was available for an extended period of time.

**Emergency Water Sources**

**Ice Cubes**: Melt them for quick use

**Bath tubs**: If you anticipate a disaster, you can fill your bath tub with water. This water can be used as an extra source of drinking water, or for sanitary purposes. If stored for extended periods, be sure to purify it.

**Hot water tanks:** Most homes have at least a 40 gallon water tank with clean, usable water. To access the water in your hot water tank, first turn off the electric or gas supply to the water heater. Turn off the gas at the intake valve or turn off the electricity at the circuit breaker, or unplug the unit. Open the drain at the bottom of the tank to retrieve the water. Do not turn on the gas or electricity when the tank is empty. When the water in the tank is refilled, you can then reactivate the gas or electric for heating.

**Pipes**: To use the water in your pipes, open (turn on) the faucet at the highest point in your house. This lets air into the plumbing system. Now you can drain the water from the pipes through the lowest faucet in the house. If the main water valve is closed, be sure that gas used to heat the water is turned off to prevent overheating.

**Water beds:** These can hold up to 400 gallons, but some water beds contain toxic chemicals that are not fully removed by many purifiers.

If you designate a water bed in your home as an emergency resource, drain it yearly and refill it with fresh water containing two ounces of bleach per 120 gallons.

**Swimming pools**: Pools can provide thousands of gallons of extra usable water if needed. This is a good source of water to use for personal hygiene and cleaning but it is not safe to drink without purification. If you need to drink it, be sure to boil it first. Pools should be covered when not in use to protect the water supply.

**Toilets**: Your toilet tank contains usable water that can be used as a last resort. If you must use toilet water, use the water in the top tank. Do not use the bowl water. Always boil the water before use and be sure the tank does not contain any chemicals.

Remember, if water service is not available your toilet will not flush. Having extra water on hand from a source such as your bath tub will allow you to continue to use your toilet. Simply add water to the tank to make the toilet work as normal. Another option would be the utilization of a camping toilet.

**Other Water Sources**: Rainwater, snow, rivers, streams, ponds and lakes, and natural springs. Avoid using water with any floating material, or an odor or dark color. Do not drink flood water as it may be contaminated. Natural water sources should be purified before drinking because they often contain bacteria that can make you sick.

**Purifying Water**

Water purification can be accomplished by boiling water in a clean container for about 5 minutes. Be sure to let it cool before drinking and keep the container covered while it is cooling. Boiled water will taste better if you restore oxygen by pouring the water back and forth between two clean containers. This will also improve the taste of stored water.

You can also purchase water purification tablets. These are available at most stores that sell sporting goods or camping supplies.

Be sure to follow the instructions provided on the package. Water purification tablets should be included in every emergency supply kit.

*Household bleach can also be used to kill microorganisms.*

To purify water with bleach, use only regular household liquid bleach that contains 5.25 to 6.0 percent sodium hypochlorite (this should be noted on the label).

Do not use scented bleaches, color safe bleaches, or bleaches with added cleaners. Use bleach from a newly opened or unopened bottle, because the potency of bleach diminishes over time.

Add 16 drops (1/8 teaspoon) of bleach per gallon of water, stir, and let stand for 30 minutes. The water should have a slight bleach odor. If it doesn't, then repeat the dosage and let stand for another 15 minutes. If it still does not smell of chlorine, discard it and find another source of water.

Emergency water supply packets are also an option. These are sealed packs of small amounts of water. They have a longer shelf life than bottled water, usually lasting up to 5 years.

**Food**

A 3 day supply of non-perishable food is recommended to have on hand (per person). You should select foods that do not require water, cooking or refrigeration. Items such as canned goods are excellent to keep stored (be sure to have a can opener also). If there is no power in your home, you should consume your perishable items first. Simple preparation is the key to successful planning.

You should have a supply of healthy foods available that will give your energy and nutrients. You should also have comfort foods such as your favorite snacks or candy on hand. During stressful events, these items may help you feel better.

**Other food items to consider**

Protein / Fruit / Energy Bars

Dry Cereal

Vitamins

Supplements

Crackers

Be sure to include food for infants and your pets.

You can also consider purchasing military type "ready to eat" meals (also known as M.R.E'.s). These are available at military surplus stores or camping supply centers.

Consider growing a garden at your home. You can have a supply of fresh fruits and vegetables if needed.

**Cooking Without a Power Source**

If gas and electric service are not available in your home, you will need a heat source to prepare your food or boil water. Consider using a barbecue grill or a camping stove. Both require fuel such as wood, charcoal or propane. Be sure to have an adequate amount of fuel prior to a disaster. Don't wait until the last minute to stock up.

Never use these cooking appliances inside a home. Be sure you know how to properly operate them before use. Be sure they are properly ventilated while being used.

**First Aid Kit**

**Your basic first aid supplies should include the following:**

**Sterile Dressings**: Use to cover wounds and stop bleeding.

**Antibiotic and burn ointment**: Use these to prevent infection in wounds and burns.

**Adhesive bandages**: Keep a variety of sizes on hand to treat a variety of wounds.

**Other important medical supplies to have:** Scissors, Medical Tape, Tweezers, Petroleum Jelly, Latex or other sterile gloves, eye wash solution.

**Prescription medications and supplies**: Do not wait until you run out of your prescriptions. Keep an adequate supply of medication in case you do not have access to a pharmacy if evacuated. Stores may be destroyed or inaccessible.

**Non-Prescription Medication**: Keep a supply of pain relievers, anti-diarrhea medication, laxatives and antacids.

**Radio**: A portable radio is good to have so you can monitor news broadcasts or emergency alerts. Be sure to have batteries on hand. You can also purchase radios that are wind up or solar powered so you do not need batteries.

**NOAA Weather Radio:** Consider purchasing one of these radios. You can program the radio to receive emergency warnings for your specific area from the National Weather Service. These are "all hazards" radios that will provide you with the most comprehensive information during an event. They are available for purchase at most department stores.

**Flashlights**: Everyone in your home should have one. Keep a supply of fresh batteries for the lights. Be sure the batteries are the correct size and type for your lights. You can also consider purchasing wind up flashlights that do not require batteries.

**Candles**: These can be an efficient source of lighting, but be sure to have matches or a lighter also. Do not leave candles unattended while burning.

**Glow Sticks:** Also known as "chem-lights", these are very useful to have in your kit. Glow sticks provide a non-flammable, heatless light source. Good quality sticks give off 8 – 12 hours of bright light. White sticks can be used for emergency lighting. Other colors could be used to signal help if needed. These are inexpensive and have an excellent shelf life.

**Blankets**: If heating is not available you should have extra blankets or a sleeping bag to keep warm. Emergency blankets are another option. Made of Mylar, emergency blankets come in compact pocket sized carry cases. When opened, they are large enough to wrap a person. These blankets can retain up to 90% of a person's body heat. They can also serve as a temporary shelter when outside. Because of their bright sliver color, they can also be used for emergency signaling.

**Extra Clothing**: Be prepared for varying weather conditions and damaged or wet clothes. Have at least one change of clothing for each person in your emergency kit appropriate for your climate.

**Tools**: Duct tape, a tarp, hammer, screw driver, wrench, pliers, and fire extinguisher. Every emergency kit should have tools in case some minor repairs are required.

**Additional Items**

Toilet paper

Infant diapers / wet wipes

Feminine supplies

Deodorant

Toothbrush / toothpaste

Garbage bags

Insect repellent

## Money

Consider having some cash. If there is no power, ATM's and store credit card readers will not work. Electronic transactions will not be an option. If you are lucky enough to have access to shopping in a disaster, merchants will most likely only accept cash.

## Entertainment

It is also important to have something to keep you and your family occupied. Have some books, toys or games available, especially for children. If your children enjoy electronic games, be sure to have batteries for those too.

The items for your emergency kit should be kept together in a carrying case that is easily accessible. You can also make a smaller kit to be carried in a car. Be sure to update the items in your kit as the needs of your family change. Also be sure to check the expiration dates of items in your kits to maintain a fresh supply. Be sure everyone in your family knows where your emergency kit is located.

## Backup Power Options

Consider the purchase of a power generator. Generators are usually gas powered and can provide many hours of electricity. Some are small and portable, intended for light use. Others are large and can fully power homes or businesses. If you have critical power requirements such as the use of life sustaining medical devices or computer systems, a generator can be invaluable. Contact your local hardware store for more information about generators.

Solar power is another option for disaster planning. Solar panels use the power of sunlight to create energy. Solar panels come in a variety of sizes depending on your energy needs. Solar can be an expensive option, but having self-generating power can save you money over time. Solar power also helps the environment as it does not create any harmful emissions.

## More Important Preparedness Tips

Designate a local contact and a third party contact out of state. If someone is out of the disaster area, all parties can check in if they become separated during the incident. Make sure everyone knows who the contact is, and the telephone number. Keep the emergency numbers in a wallet or backpack.

Make copies of your ID cards, credit cards, insurance policies and birth certificates. Keep your important documents in a portable flame resistant and water proof container. Keep your originals or copies in a ready pack that you can take with you if you need to leave your home in a hurry. Don't forget to include information for your family members and pets.

Create an inventory of personal possessions. Document the serial numbers and model numbers of valuable items if possible. Photographs or video recordings of your property are also great ideas. Keep these protected along with your other important documents.

## Disaster Ready Patrol Vehicles

Every officer should carry personal emergency supplies in their patrol car. If you plan to respond to other jurisdictions, it is critical to have supplies with you as they may not be available where you are going. The items on the following list are fairly inexpensive and can make you more comfortable in severe weather or a disaster situation.

**Weather Gear:** Dress for the weather. This includes rain gear, hats, covers, jackets, boots and gloves.

**Emergency Blankets:** These are compact and fit easily into any duty bag. They can provide warmth if you are stranded or they can also serve as a blanket for injured in a cold weather environment,

**Flashlight:** This is common sense. Every officer should always carry a flashlight. It is better to carry 2, should the first one fail.

**First Aid Kit:** First aid kits should be carried for your own protection. Cuts, scrapes, insect bites and other minor injuries can be treat by yourself in the field.

**Latex Gloves:** You should always have a supply of latex or or other type of protective gloves. They are important to minimize contact blood borne contamination, but you can also use them when handling narcotics, weapons or other evidence to prevent fingerprint contamination..

**N95 Particle Masks:** These are handy to wear in a dusty or dirty environment. They can also provide some protection against other airborne contaminants.

**Fire Extinguisher:** Carry to put out minor fires.

**Eye Protection:** When working in debris or dusty environments, wear goggles or protective eye wear.

**Cell Phone:** 2 way radios may not be active. Always have a backup communication source.

**Fix-A-Flat:** Sometimes it's just not an option to wait for a tow truck. Carrying a quick fix tire sealant may get you out of a dangerous situation.

**Maps / GPS:** During a disaster, street signs may be missing. Be sure you can find you way around, especially in other jurisdictions!

**Hand Sanitizer:** Prevent the spread of germs when soap and water are not readily available.

**Cones or Flares:** Have an adequate supply to be able to effectively close roads or redirect traffic.

**Helmet:** Protect your head from falling objects or other hazards.

**Tyvek Suit:** When working in a contaminated or dirty environment, wear a protective suit.

**Crime Scene Tape:** Use to limit access to certain areas.

**Sunscreen:** Officers should always carry sunscreen lotion or spray. Wear it in the summer and winter to protect your-self. Be sure to use an SPF (Sun Protection Factor) of 30 or higher for maximum protection.

**Emergency Response Guidebook:** This is a book provided by the US Dept. of Transportation. It provides information on hazardous materials. The book is free to all public safety agencies. Be able to identify hazards if needed. To obtain copies, check with your agency administrator or visit: http://hazmat.dot.gov

**Note:** Supervisor vehicles should carry extras of these items.

Here are some other good items to have either in your patrol car or a supervisor vehicle:

**Duct Tape:** Allows for a quick fix if needed.

**Additional Radios:** Having an extra radio or two will allow you to have a backup if one is damaged. It could also allow you to pass one on to another agency for inter-agency talk if needed.

**Jump Box:** Don't be left stranded. Have a way of jump starting vehicles with dead batteries.

**Shovel (Army E-tool):** This will aid in digging out stuck vehicles, or it could aid in searches or rescues.

**Spray Paint:** Use to mark roadways or use for searches to mark areas checked.

**Rope:** May be needed for rescues or tie downs.

**Cooler:** Be sure you and other officers are hydrated. When working extended scenes, be sure to have water or other drinks accessible.

## Station Preparedness

Refer to the section on emergency supplies. At the very least, you should have an emergency supply of water available. If your station is going to be the location of your community's emergency operations center, it is essential that you are well supplied. This includes all of the life sustaining items such as food, medical supplies and other needs. Consider the needs of dispatchers or office staff that may not be able to leave for an extended period of time in an emergency situation.

Officers and staff may need to rest, so consider having cots, blankets or other comfort items available. At an individual level, you should always keep a spare uniform in your locker. Also keep extra pairs of socks, underwear and if possible, boots.

## Weapons

If responding outside your jurisdiction, you should still carry your issued duty weapon unless your agency policy prohibits it. Law enforcement officers are authorized to carry firearms nationwide. In a disaster scenario, you will be working under the policies and procedures of the jurisdiction you are in. Be sure to familiarize yourself with these policies upon arrival. Carry any needed supplies with you. This includes ammunition, cleaning kits, batteries, etc. as they may not be available at your location.

If flying to your location, there are special considerations. Your weapon will generally be checked in with your baggage. Contact the airline you will be flying on for detailed information. You can also contact the TSA for more information.

When traveling, you should wear your standard uniform which identifies you as a law enforcement officer. Be sure to carry identification with you also (ID Card with photo, badge, etc.).

**Always check in with the Incident Commander upon arrival at your destination.**

# CHAPTER 6

## Managing Stress

Recovering from a disaster is usually a gradual process. Physical safety is always a primary issue, but mental health often gets overlooked. This section offers some general advice on steps you can take after disaster strikes in order to begin getting your home, your community, and your life back to normal.

Everyone who sees or experiences a disaster will be affected by it in some way. It is perfectly normal to feel concerned or anxious about your own safety and the safety of your family and friends. Sadness, confusion, grief, anger and frustration are normal emotional reactions to an abnormal event. Public safety officers don't like to admit when there is a problem. Stress is a common problem following a disaster or other traumatic incident. You need to recognize and understand that stress and worry are normal parts of what you do. Be aware of the signs and symptoms so you manage stress before it gets out of hand.

How you deal with your stress will determine how you get through the recovery process. It is often easy to overlook emotional stress, as everyone experiences disaster differently. Anyone, regardless of age or background can be affected by stress. Some people will openly express feelings, but others may contain them. It is extremely important that you recognize the symptoms of someone in emotional distress. By recognizing the symptoms, you may be able to help get a life back to normal. Persons showing signs of stress should seek assistance as soon as possible to minimize the effects. The sooner you seek treatment, the sooner you'll get things back to normal.

## Symptoms of Stress

Difficulty with communicating

Excessive anxiety

Having trouble sleeping or having nightmares

Easily angered or frustrated

Increased use of drugs or alcohol

Limited attention span

Poor or declining work performance

Persistent headaches or stomach problems

Tunnel vision or muffled hearing

Little or no energy

Disorientation or confusion

Difficulty concentrating on simple tasks

Loss of appetite or overeating

General depression or sadness

Feelings of hopelessness

Severe mood swings.

Guilt or self-doubt that overwhelms you

If you or someone you know has these symptoms, there are things you can do. Talk with someone and tell them about your feelings. Discussing your feelings can help you recover faster.

Although it may be difficult, it is important to do so. Do not be embarrassed about seeking help from a professional counselor who deals with disaster related stress. Getting help when you need it is not a weakness. You can get counseling help from community groups, local faith-based organizations, volunteer agencies, or professional counselors.

You can also speak with your family physician, as there may also be other underlying medical issues related to the stress. Post-traumatic stress disorder (PTSD) is quite common, as well as depression. The good thing is that these are treatable. FEMA, state and local governments may also provide crisis counseling assistance in areas affected by disaster.

You do not have to be directly involved with a disaster to experience disaster stress. Symptoms of second hand exposure can come from media coverage or worry. People who experience a disaster indirectly can show the same symptoms as those who are directly affected. Even just planning for disaster can be stressful. Worry can easily overwhelm you if you let it.

Dealing with your emotional stress is just as important as making an emergency kit. You can improve your own physical and emotional well-being by eating healthy foods, getting adequate rest and exercising on a regular basis. Take time to relax. Try to get back to a normal routine after a disaster. Spend quality time with family and friends and limit demanding activities. Try to do things that make you happy.

**Children and Disasters**

Children are of special concern in the aftermath of disasters. Disasters can be traumatic events for children, even if they were not directly affected by it. Children may be more prone to fear and anxiety than adults because they do not understand why disasters occur. Educate children about the different types of disasters. If a child has questions about a disaster, answer them truthfully. Remind them it is okay to be scared. Be sure to comfort them to ease the anxiety. It is important for adults to discuss feelings about disaster with children.

Children's anxiety levels can increase by simply hearing parents or teachers talk about events. Seeing images of disaster on television can add to the anxiety. It is very important for parents and teachers to recognize and understand the symptoms of emotional stress.

Kids are very observant. They will notice fear, anxiety and sadness in adults. Parents can help make disasters less stressful for children by discussing their own thoughts, feelings and fears. If parents share feelings, they can help children while managing their own feelings and fears. Some children may not want to talk about their feelings. Offer other ways of expressing feelings such as drawing a picture or telling a story. Remain positive and validate the feelings expressed. A major fear of those involved in an incident is that it will happen again.

Children can experience many of the same stress symptoms as adults. In addition to fear and sadness, children may also demonstrate behavioral problems. Young children may experience bed wetting, sleep problems, and separation anxiety. Older children may show anger, aggression and withdrawal. Both younger and older children may have difficulty with performance in school. Emotional reactions to disasters are often brief for most children, but some may be at risk for longer lasting psychological issues based on other major risk factors or history.

## Direct Exposure or Involvement

Fear and anxiety are to be expected in children. Those who directly experience events such as sustaining personal injury, witnessing injuries or death or being involved in a life threatening experience will have a higher risk of emotional distress and long term issues. It is critical that these children be monitored for problems. If a child experiences the loss of a friend or family member due to a disaster, it can be even more of a traumatic emotional event. Kids may also have an increased worry in mom or dad is involved in the rescue response.

## On-Going Stress

Being evacuated from home, losing personal property and having to stay in temporary housing can be a major shock to a child. Children may not understand why things are changing. They will be in unfamiliar situations with people they may not know. This is very uncomfortable for adults, but more so for kids. Observed parental stress will add to the emotional problems of children.

Post disaster anxiety and stress in children can increase through reminders of the event. For those directly involved in a disaster, certain triggers can bring back memories of the event. Photos, media coverage, sirens, storms or other related reminders can bring back upsetting feelings. Children with prior history of traumatic events or severe stress may have an increase in these feelings. Try to be aware of these triggers and limit them as best you can until the child can better handle their emotions.

Depending on the risk factors above, most distressing responses in children are often temporary. In the absence of a life threatening event, personal injury, or the loss of loved ones, most emotional symptoms will go away with time. Seek professional help if they do not seem to be going away.

Parents are the first line of support for children coping with disaster. Engage your family and involve children in drills and the emergency planning process. Let them know you have a plan to keep them safe. Reassure them that schools and other adults are also developing plans to keep everyone safe.

Let them know you are doing everything you can to take care of them and that everything will be okay. Just as with adults, children need to learn to prepare for disasters. Reassure them you are doing what is needed by planning and creating an emergency kit. Allow them to participate in the process.

Remain calm and stay positive. Try to show that you are in control and prepared. Your confidence and emotional well-being will extend to your children.

Take your children to visit a police or fire station. Let them meet rescuers and allow them to learn about rescue equipment. All children are curious about these things. Sometimes children are afraid of police or firefighters because they have never encountered them up close. Building trust can be a major step in overcoming anxiety about emergencies. In addition, it may help to reassure them someone is there watching out when disasters happen.

# CHAPTER 7

## Natural Threats

Weather threats are a danger every one of us will face at some time in our lives. The good thing about weather events is that you will usually have warning before they strike. In the event of a severe weather situation or other threat, watches or warnings will be issued. Having advance notice will give you time to prepare or react. Dispatchers should always be monitoring weather threats. Officers can also monitor threats with a portable weather radio.

If you fail to act upon the warnings, you may face danger. Officers take precautions for many things on duty, but many fail to respond to the dangers hazardous weather presents. Those who do not listen to warnings are the ones who usually suffer the most. With proper precautions, it is possible to make it through a hazardous natural event without incident.

***Know your warnings and be sure to follow them.***

**Watch**: Watches are issued when weather conditions exist that <u>could</u> create a hazard. You should be aware of the potential hazard and begin to take precautions.

**Warning**: A warning is issued when a specific threat <u>is</u> occurring. If a warning is issued, you may be in immediate danger. You should follow the instructions given to protect yourself.

**Reminder:** Weather radios save lives. Everyone should have one!

The following pages will guide you through the dangers of specific natural hazards.

# Avalanche

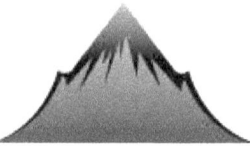

Avalanches are large amounts of rapidly moving snow that occur in mountainous terrain. Avalanches are made of snow which differentiates them from landslides. Avalanches are always caused by external stress on the snow pack. They claim more than 150 lives worldwide every year. Thousands of other people have been injured or partially buried.

To prevent avalanches, do not ski, hike or snowmobile in avalanche prone areas. Assess hazardous areas and consult with area mapping agencies to determine your risk before entering dangerous areas. If you are caught in an avalanche, try to take cover behind large trees or rocks. Crouch low, cover your mouth and nose and turn away from the avalanche. If you are caught in the snow pack, thrust and kick upward to get to the surface of the snow. Many avalanche deaths are caused by suffocation. As the snow pack slows, pull your arms and hands toward your face to create an air space.

When the slide stops, try to remain calm. Yell for help if rescuers are near, but conserve your energy. Try to thrust an arm to the surface and try to dig yourself out.

For more information, consult local guides for maximum safety. If you are planning a backcountry adventure, carry a portable shovel and adequate supplies with you. You can also carry a collapsible ski pole probe. These are poles that can be pieced together to aid in finding a buried victim. Avalanche beacons can also be carried. These are transmitters that emit a signal to help rescuers locate trapped victims. Always let someone know where you'll be, and when you'll be back. Avoid back country travel when you are alone.

# Blackouts / Power Outages

Blackouts, or power outages can be caused by a variety of factors. They can be caused by faults, solar storms or other problems at power stations. They may also be caused by damage to power transmission lines (poles and wires being knocked down or struck by lightning), overloaded power grids, or short circuits. Most power outages are only temporary, lasting just a few minutes or hours. In a large disaster, the outages may last longer.

To prepare for outages, have a working flashlight with good batteries accessible. Candles are also a good idea. Remember to have matches or a lighter. Glow sticks are a great option. They provide many hours of safe bright light and do not require fuel or batteries.

Blackouts can cause panic in the community. It can also lead to looting or other crimes. Maintain a higher level of vigilance when there is a power outage. Increase your patrols to ease the concerns of citizens and to watch for criminal activity. Monitor intersections as traffic lights may also be out. Try to have traffic control options available before a power outage. This includes portable stop signs, flares, cones or other ways to control traffic.

# Earthquakes

Earthquakes are caused by the movement of plates deep within the Earth's surface. These plates move constantly and rub against each other. The plates occasionally shift with great force, causing a quake. A fault line is the area where the rocks are sliding past each other. The movement in the fault lines often can cause cracks in the Earth's surface. Some fault lines are more active than others, such as the San Andreas Fault in southern California. Earthquakes can often trigger Tsunami's.

There are more than a million recorded earthquakes each year. Earthquakes can occur anywhere. Most people think of California when you mention earthquakes. However, in 1811 and 1812, three quakes believed to be some of the largest and most violent in US history were actually centered in an area of southeast Missouri known as New Madrid.

The earthquake forcibly shook the ground in a 50,000 square mile area. With minimal communication and a sparse population, there was no way of knowing how many people were injured or killed, or how many structures were destroyed. Seismograph equipment was not yet in use, so there was no way of knowing the true intensity. There were reports of church bells ringing in Philadelphia because of the shaking. Shaking was also said to have been felt in Boston, New York and Norfolk, Virginia.

The New Madrid Fault is still active today. It is believed the area of southeast Missouri will be the center of a major earthquake sometime in the near future. If a major quake should occur, the urban areas of Memphis Tennessee, Little Rock Arkansas and St. Louis Missouri could be severely affected. Earthquakes can strike anywhere. You should be aware of the hazards, no matter where you live.

## What to do if an earthquake strikes

If you are inside during an earthquake, remain calm, drop to the ground and seek cover under something such as a sturdy desk or table. Try to hang on to something. Protect your head with a pillow or your hands. Stay where you are and do not try to move around until the shaking is over. If you are outside seek an open area away from buildings, trees and power lines. Beware of falling debris.

Check for injuries then inspect your structure after the shaking has stopped. Be aware of aftershocks that may occur. If your location is damaged, stay out of it until it has been inspected by a professional. Beware of downed power lines, damaged utilities and other structural damage or dangerous debris.

Falling objects are a threat during earthquakes. To better prepare for an earthquake, bolt book shelves or other tall furniture to a wall. Place heavy or large items on lower shelves. Secure cupboards and cabinets with latches that prevent them from opening during a quake. Do not hang pictures or other items over your bed or chairs. Brace hanging light fixtures. Secure your water heater by strapping it to wall studs.

# Floods

Floods are the most common natural disaster in the United States. Flooding can occur when there are heavy rains or excessive melting snow. Floods can also occur from high ocean tides, improper urban storm drainage, damaged levees or broken dams. Rivers, streams and lakes may overflow due to the excessive water amounts. At risk locations include coastal regions, areas adjacent to rivers, streams, or lakes, dry river beds and low lying areas such as valleys. On average, floods kill over 140 people each year and cause over $6 billion dollars in property damage. Flooding can occur in any part of our nation at any time of the year.

If flooding is anticipated, go to higher ground. Flash flooding is also a serious risk. If heavy rains are expected, avoid dry river beds, creeks, streams and valleys during a storm. Flood water can move rapidly and without warning. It may not be raining where you are, but water can flow from far away, especially in mountainous areas. Dry areas can turn into raging rivers in only a matter of minutes.

Do NOT attempt to drive through flooded areas. It is important to close roads or bridges that may be underwater. Only 6 inches of moving water can knock you off your feet. 2 feet of moving water will cause your car to float. Water levels are often difficult to judge. Don't take the chance of driving through deep water. If a road appears to be flooded, take another route. Pay attention to closed road signs. Always have an alternate response route.

If your home is prone to flooding, raise up items such as furnaces, electrical boxes and water heaters. Move furniture, electronics and valuables to a higher area of your home.

# Excessive Heat

Law enforcement officers are prone to heat related issues due to the nature of our work. We wear body armor, heavy uniforms, 20+ pounds of gear and we work out in the sun for extended periods. We overload ourselves with coffee and other caffeinated beverages when we should be drinking water. Heat exhaustion and heat stroke are serious conditions caused by exposure to excessive heat. The human body can normally regulate its temperature in hot weather by sweating. In excessive heat your body can't keep up and becomes overloaded.

Infants, young children, the elderly and overweight people are the most vulnerable to heat related problems. Heat related illnesses are common, but they can be prevented. The easiest way to prevent heat problems is to stay hydrated by drinking water and avoid excessive time in the heat. It does not take long to become dehydrated. It is very important to drink water before, during after being exposed to hot weather. Do your best to stay cool.

Two main effects of excessive heat exposure are Heat Stroke and Heat Exhaustion. Both can be life threatening if not treated.

## Warning Signs of Heat Stroke

An extremely high body temperature (above 103°F)

Red, hot, and dry skin (no sweating)

Rapid, strong pulse

Throbbing headache

Dizziness / Nausea

Confusion

Unconsciousness

Heat stroke is a very serious condition. These symptoms may be signs of a life threatening emergency. If you witness someone with these symptoms, seek professional medical assistance immediately.

Move the victim to a shady area. Cool the victim rapidly, using whatever methods you can. For example, immerse the victim in a tub of cool water; place the person in a cool shower; spray the victim with cool water from a garden hose; sponge the person with cool water; or if the humidity is low, wrap the victim in a cool, wet sheet and fan the patient vigorously.

Monitor body temperature and continue cooling efforts until the body temperature drops to 101-102°F.

If emergency medical personnel are delayed, call a hospital emergency room for further instructions. If communications are not available, do your best to keep the patient cool until help arrives.

Do not give the victim any beverages that contain alcohol. Allow them to drink cool water if they are alert and conscious. Do not attempt to give liquids to an unconscious person.

**Heat Exhaustion**

Heat exhaustion can develop after several days of exposure to high temperatures and inadequate or unbalanced replacement of fluids. Those most prone to heat exhaustion are elderly people, those with high blood pressure, and those working or exercising in a hot environment. Hundreds of people die from heat exhaustion each year because they failed to take proper care of themselves.

If you need to work or exercise outside, do so during the early morning or late night when temperatures are coolest. Beware of warnings signs to prevent heat related health problems before they get worse.

## Warning signs of heat exhaustion

Heavy sweating

Paleness

Muscle cramps

Tiredness

Weakness

Dizziness

Headache

Nausea or vomiting

Fainting

The skin may be cool and moist. The pulse rate will be fast and weak, and breathing will be fast and shallow. If heat exhaustion is untreated, it may progress to heat stroke. Seek medical attention if symptoms worsen or if they last longer than one hour.

It is important to try to cool the body. Drink cool, nonalcoholic beverages and seek an air-conditioned environment.

Wear lightweight clothing.

Get adequate rest.

Take a cool shower, bath, or sponge bath.

Have your air conditioning system inspected regularly to ensure it running at peak efficiency. Also consider the use of fans to improve comfort and reduce cooling costs.

# Hurricanes

Hurricanes are huge storms that form over warm ocean waters. These storms can be up to 600 miles across and can have winds averaging 75 – 200 miles per hour. Storms gain strength over the open ocean. As they approach land, they dump huge amounts of rain and can cause substantial wind damage. Flooding is a result of high tides and excessive rain. The storms lose power as they move ashore but often leave a trail of destruction.

A hurricane watch is issued when conditions exist with sustained winds of 74 mph or greater in your area within the next 36 hours. A hurricane warning is issued when hurricane conditions are expected in your area within 24 hours. Flood warnings or watches may be issued as well as small craft advisories. If you are on a boat you should get to land or remain on shore during a warning period.

If you anticipate a hurricane, secure any items in your yard that could blow away or cause damage. Board up or protect windows. If flooding is expected, go further inland or go to higher ground. You may be required to evacuate from locations in the path of the storm or in flood prone areas. Monitor warnings for instructions. Follow directions if you are told to evacuate. Do not drive through flooded areas and be aware of debris in the roadway. Maintain extra vigilance for looters in storm damaged or vacated areas.

# Landslides

Landslides can be caused by a variety of unstable material (mud, rocks or other debris) on a sloped surface. Mudslides caused by heavy rains or snow often cause problems. Gravity may cause loose rocks to fall, causing a slide. Groundwater, erosion or loss of vegetation on slopes can also cause a normally stable area to become unstable.

Homes that are built on or near slopes and cliffs are more prone to slides. If you live in a landslide prone area, contact a professional (civil engineer) for advice on landslide management. There may corrective measures you can make to prevent problems.

If your home or building is in the path of an impending landslide, evacuate immediately. If you cannot evacuate, get on the floor, curl into a tight ball and protect your head. Try to get out of the path of a landslide. After a slide, check your home for structural damage. Also check the area around your home for erosion damage and broken utility lines. Monitor warnings for instructions during a storm or during a landslide event.

Use caution when traveling through areas where landslides may occur. If a road is not accessible, find another route. If roads are damaged or impassible, close the road to prevent drivers from entering.

# Thunderstorms

About 2,000 thunderstorms occur every day somewhere on the Earth, causing about 100 strikes of cloud to ground lightning every second. They can occur during any season and in any location. Thunderstorms are formed by rapidly rising unstable warm moist air. These storms can cause strong wind gusts, heavy rains and hail. The biggest danger in a thunderstorm comes from lightning.

Lightning is a large discharge of electricity. Within a thundercloud, small bits of ice bump into each other as they move around in the atmosphere. Lightning is believed to be caused by the collisions of these ice crystals. As they collide, they create an electric charge. After a while, the whole cloud fills up with electrical charges. The positive charges (protons) form at the top of the cloud and the negative charges (electrons) form at the bottom of the cloud. Because opposites attract, this causes a positive charge to build up on the ground beneath the cloud. The electrical charge on the ground concentrates around anything that rises up, such as mountains, people, or trees. The charge coming up from these points eventually connects with a charge reaching down from the clouds thus creating a lightning bolt. A lightning bolt can travel at speeds up to 22,000 miles per hour (36,000 km/h) and has a temperature of about 50,000 degrees (F).

Thunder is caused by lightning. When a lightning bolt travels from the cloud to the ground it actually opens up a small hole in the air, called a channel. Once the light has gone through, the air collapses back in and creates a sound wave that we hear as thunder. The reason we see lightning before we hear thunder is because light travels faster than sound.

Thunder can typically be heard within about 15 miles of its source. Lightning can be seen from as far away as 100 miles.

If you can hear thunder, you may be in danger of getting struck by lightning. If you are outside during a storm, seek shelter immediately. If you are outside during a storm and you can feel your hair stand on end or your skin starts to tingle, lightning may be about to strike. Get down on your hands and knees and keep your head tucked in. Do not lie flat, because it can give the lightning a better chance of striking you.

On average, lightning kills more people each year than hurricanes and tornadoes. You can estimate how far away a storm is by counting the number of seconds between when you see the lightning and hear the thunder. Take the number of seconds then divide by 5. This will tell you the storm distance in miles. For example: If you counted 10 seconds between the lightning and the thunder, the lightning would be 2 miles away.

**During a Thunderstorm**

Seek cover inside a building, home or other suitable shelter until the storm has passed. Try to avoid being outside during lightning.

Shut off electrical devices to prevent damage from power surges. Protect electronics with a surge protection device.

Do not swim during a storm. If you are in water, get out immediately. If you are on a boat, get to shore immediately.

Do not take a shower or a bath during a storm. Electricity can be carried through water and metal pipes.

Do not use wired telephones because lightning can be carried through the wires.

# Tornadoes

A tornado is a violently rotating column of air extending from a thunderstorm to the ground. Most tornadoes form from thunderstorms. For a tornado to form there must be warm, moist air mixing with cool, dry air. When the two air masses meet, instability is created in the atmosphere. A change in wind direction and an increase in wind speed with increasing height create an invisible, horizontal spinning effect in the lower atmosphere. The rotating air tilts from horizontal to vertical as air rises. An area of rotation, 2-6 miles wide, then extends through much of the storm. Tornadoes can form within this area of rotation. A funnel cloud is a spinning vortex extending from the cloud, but it does not reach the ground. A tornado is a funnel that contacts the ground.

Tornadoes are capable of causing massive destruction in a short period of time. Winds in a tornado can reach speeds of up to 300 miles per hour. In an average year, over 800 tornadoes occur in the United States. Tornadoes can happen at any time of the year and in any climate. Tornadoes have been recorded on every continent with the exception of Antarctica.

Tornado watches are issued when weather conditions are present that can spawn tornadoes. Warnings are issued when a funnel cloud or tornado has been spotted by a trained storm spotter or on weather radar. You can watch for tornadoes while you are on patrol. Look for a lowering cloud base and cloud rotation. Watch for small funnels, or "ropes" forming in the cloud. If you see funnels or an actual tornado on the ground, notify your dispatcher immediately. Time is critical when a tornado is on the ground. Rapid notification and alerts can save lives.

If a tornado warning is issued, seek shelter immediately. Go to a designated tornado shelter, or the lowest area of your home or building. Remain there until the storm has passed. If you are in an automobile, get to an indoor shelter. Do not try to out drive the storm. If you are outside with no shelter, go to a low lying area such as a ditch and lie flat. Cover your head for protection. Do not seek cover under bridges. Stay away from trees or power lines.

If you do not have access to a basement, go to an interior room without windows, such as a bathroom or closet. You can also seek cover under a sturdy table or desk. Stay away from windows and doors.

If you live in a mobile home, get out and seek cover in a more suitable shelter. Mobile homes can be damaged or destroyed in only a minor tornado.

If possible, either have on sturdy shoes, or have them accessible if you are in the path of a storm. Also, try to keep gloves handy. If there is damage and debris after a tornado, you'll want to protect your feet and hands. It's also a good idea to cover your mouth and nose. Try to minimize breathing in dust and other contaminants. This can be done with the use of respirators, or something as simple as a bandana or t-shirt.

**Note**: In areas served by tornado sirens, you should be aware that they are only meant to be heard outdoors. If you are outside when you hear a tornado siren, get inside immediately. For notification when indoors, your best protection for warnings would be a weather radio, television or regular AM/FM type radio.

# Tsunamis

A Tsunami is a series of large waves caused by sudden displacements in the ocean floor (an earthquake), landslides or volcanoes. These waves can be very large and can submerge coastal cities causing massive destruction and death. Waves can travel in the open sea at speeds of up to 450 miles per hour. They can reach heights of 100 feet tall. Tsunamis occur most frequently in the Pacific Ocean region, but they can occur in any large lake, sea or ocean. Tsunamis are sometimes referred to a "tidal waves", but this is an inaccurate term as tsunamis have nothing to do with tidal movements of the Earth.

If you are in a coastal area when an earthquake occurs or if a tsunami warning is issued, stay calm and get to higher ground as soon as possible. If you cannot get to higher ground, go to the highest floor of building.

Tsunamis are preceded by a rapidly receding tide. The low tide is created by the growing wave further out at sea.  If you are on a beach and the tide appears to be receding rapidly, or changing in an untimely pattern, listen for warnings and get to higher ground immediately.

Though it's not common, Tsunamis can occur in lakes and rivers.

# Winter Storms

A winter storm (also known as a Blizzard) forms when two air masses of different temperatures and moisture levels collide. Winter storms usually form when a cold, dry, Arctic air mass moves south and interacts with a warm, moist air mass moving north from the Gulf of Mexico. Winter storms can cause many problems. Extreme cold, heavy snow and ice are a few of the threats caused by these storms. Reduced visibility, slippery roads and other hazardous conditions can also occur. The best thing to do is stay home unless you absolutely need to leave.

Winter storm watches or warnings may be issued when the threat exists for extreme cold, heavy snow or ice.

Winter storms are usually predictable, so you can prepare for them. Stock up on needed supplies before the storm arrives. Winter storms often knock out power. Blizzards can dump a large amount of snow in a short period of time. Be sure you are prepared to deal sheltering in place if you are not able to leave where you are.

Extreme cold can be very hazardous. Wear layered clothing if you'll be exposed to the cold. If temperatures warm up, you can remove clothing items. It is better to be too warm than too cold. Try to limit your exposure to extreme cold.

Gather snow and ice removal equipment in advance. Have a shovel to clear snow and rock salt to melt ice on walkways and stairs.

If traveling through areas where storms are expected, be sure to let others know where you'll be going. Check weather forecasts and try to avoid travelling during the storm. Beware of roads covered in snow, especially during drift situations. Visibility can be limited and the road may not be passable.

Always keep your car fueled with at least a half tank of gas. Keep a blanket, tire chains and snow removal equipment (shovel, snow brush and ice scraper) in your car. If your car gets stuck or stranded, stay with it. It can provide temporary shelter from the cold and will make it easier for rescuers to find you. To signal for help, tie a brightly colored cloth to your antenna or place it in the top of a rolled up window. Turn on your hazard flashers to signal others, but only when your engine is running. Using lights with the engine off will cause your battery to drain.

Use your engine and heater just long enough to take off the chill in the car. This will help conserve fuel. Have a portable emergency kit with you. Drive with care and allow more time to get where you're going. Winter driving requires extra attention. Accelerate and decelerate slowly. Be sure to allow further stopping distance on wet or slippery surfaces. You may be the best driver in the world, but unfortunately, not everyone else is. If you don't need to drive, don't. Limit your responses to only those requiring immediate attention. Accidents will always increase in severe weather. Consider taking phone reports for incidents requiring a delayed response.

Carry a cell phone with you and be sure it's charged. Be sure you always know where you are in case you need to call for help.

If you have a fire place in your home, keep an adequate supply of logs. Have your flue and chimney inspected regularly. If you have a furnace, have it checked also to keep it running at peak efficiency. Consider the use of space heaters to reduce energy costs. Insulate your attic, walls and pipes in your home or business to increase your heat efficiency.

# Wildfires

Wildfires are also known as brush fires, grass fires, forest fires, or wild land fires. They can be caused by natural sources such as lighting igniting dry vegetation. They can also be man-made, caused by arson or unintentionally by vehicles or carelessness. Areas affected by hot and dry climates are more at risk, though wildfires can occur anywhere. These fires burn millions of acres each year and cause extensive property damage. Many lives have been lost due to wildfires. On average, 4 out of 5 wildfires are human caused. Fires can spread rapidly, as they are often fueled by strong winds.

**You may not be able stop an existing wildfire, but there are some things you can do to minimize your risk.**

Allow at least a 30 foot safety zone around homes and buildings. This includes clearing dead vegetation, leaves, brush, or fallen trees and branches. Remove any combustible materials from this area. Keep your grass no taller than 2 inches. Increasing the distance of vegetation from your home will increase your fire safety. If you are not responsible for codes or fire violations, make note of hazard conditions and refer them to the appropriate fire authority.

Remove tree limbs within 15 feet of the ground. Ask your power supplier to remove branches from around power lines. Trim tree branches and shrubs that are within 15 feet of your chimney or stove pipe. Remove debris and vegetation from under decks and porches. Remove vines or other vegetation from the walls and roof of your house. Replace highly flammable vegetation in your yard with less flammable species.

Create a second safety space around your home. The second space should start at the 30 foot zone and continue out to 100 feet. Try to reduce, remove or replace flammable vegetation in this area.

Stack firewood at least 100 feet from buildings.

Store any flammable materials in approved containers away from homes and any heat sources. Keep gas grills and propane tanks at least 15 feet from homes.

Consider the use of fire resistant siding materials on your home. Materials such as stucco, metal, brick, cement shingles, concrete and rock provide good protection. Also consider using tile roofing. This is more fire resistant than wood. If remodeling, renovating or considering new construction, use fire resistant materials.

If you have time before an evacuation, place a hose with a water sprinkler on your roof. Leave the water on to help wet the area. You can also wet down areas around your home to reduce the spread of fire.

If you are evacuated, do not return to your home or property until told it is safe to do so.

**Wildfire Prevention**

A wildfire can spread very fast. If you see a small fire, notify the fire department immediately.

You can prevent wildfires by not throwing out lit cigarettes. Camping is fun, but be sure to make safe fires. Completely extinguish all camp fires before leaving.

If using off road vehicles, use a spark arrestor. This will not completely prevent fires, but it will help. Sparks or heat from a vehicle exhaust can ignite fires in dry brush and grass.

Do not use open flame grills during high risk fire times.

If "red flag" warnings are issued, use extreme care with fire. These National Weather Service warnings are usually issued during periods of drought, high winds, and low humidity. During these times, fires may be banned in certain areas.

When responding to assist with large fires, be aware of weather conditions. Winds can shift rapidly which may place you in danger. Avoid driving through fire areas. Maintain communication with fire officials to advise them of changes in your situation.

Carry a dusk mask or respirator if you will be exposed to smoke for an extended period of time. Also consider carrying an emergency fire blanket if you will frequently be exposed to wildfire situations.

# Volcanoes

There are more than 1500 active volcanoes on the Earth. 80 or more are found under the ocean waters. Volcanoes are what helped shape our planet. The largest active volcano currently is Mauna Loa in Hawaii. It measures 13,677 feet above sea level. Over 50% of the most active and dormant volcanoes are found in an area known as the "Ring of Fire". The "Ring of Fire extends along the western northern and eastern perimeter edge of the Pacific Ocean. Nearly 90% of the world's earthquakes and about 81% of the largest earthquakes on Earth occur within the ring.

Volcanoes are dangerous because they can spew burning ash into the atmosphere that can travel for thousands of miles. This is a threat, even here in the US. A west coast volcano could cause many problems in the Midwest and east coast due to the ash cloud. Flowing lava can destroy anything in its path and falling debris from the eruption can cause additional damage and injuries. If a volcano is predicted to occur, follow orders issued by authorities.

Try to avoid any areas that are downwind of the eruption. Stay out of river valleys and stay downstream of the volcano because mud flows often occur after an eruption. If you are inside your home or business, close all doors and windows. Be sure to bring in pets and children. If you are outside, seek shelter inside immediately. If you are outside and there is falling debris, get on the ground and curl up in ball. Cover your head with your hands.

Protect yourself from falling ash by wearing long-sleeved shirts and long pants. Volcanic ash can irritate your eyes and lungs. Wear a dusk mask or respirator and goggles to protect your nose, mouth and eyes. If ash accumulates on your roof, clear it off. Ash can be heavy and may cause your roof to collapse.

Although there are not many active volcanoes in the United States, there are many locations that have potential to erupt at some time in the future.

Thousands of people visit Yellowstone National Park in northwest Wyoming to see the "Old Faithful" geyser. "Old Faithful" is a regular eruption of boiling water. What many people don't know is that Yellowstone is on top of what is possibly the largest "super volcano" in the world. Super volcanoes have the potential to create a massive eruption that could cause extreme destruction and potentially alter the climate of the Earth.

In the state of Hawaii, you can witness the largest and most active volcanoes in the world. The Mauna Loa volcano is the largest on Earth by volume. The Kilauea volcano is the most active.

Volcanoes affect people in many locations around the world. If you ever encounter volcanic activity, always follow instructions provided by alert warnings. If you are told to evacuate it is in your best interest to do so.

# Chapter 8

## Man Made Threats

## Terrorism

Terrorism is defined as "The use of unlawful violence or threat of unlawful violence to induce fear; intended to coerce or to intimidate governments or societies in the pursuit of goals that are generally political, religious, or ideological." As long as man has been on the earth, there has been terrorism. There are hundreds of groups around the world who seek to cause change through violent methods. Terrorists seek to cause maximum casualties and damage in the most efficient method possible. This is usually accomplished through the use of explosives. In recent years we have seen an increase in the creativity of terrorists. Non-traditional methods such as chemical, nuclear and biological attacks have caused new fears, as well as the aircraft attacks of September 11th 2001. The way we go about our day to day lives has been changed because of terrorism.

Terrorists can work in a variety of ways. Some prefer to use psychological terrorism. This creates fear, stress and chaos without actually causing any physical destruction. It is often brought about by intimidation or hoaxes. Bomb threats are an example of psychological terrorism. Others choose more traditional methods of destruction such as the actual use of explosives or other types of weapons to inflict maximum damage or injury.

Terrorism can happen anywhere, at any time. High risk targets present more of a threat. High risk targets may include places such as government offices, schools, churches, large public gatherings, airports and other transportation facilities.

Terrorists seek opportunities to commit acts. They will often plan attacks months or years in advance. Terrorists will often scout locations and conduct surveillance. It is not uncommon for terrorists to conduct "test runs" where security will be tested to see if they will be challenged. Things that may appear strange may be indicators of something more serious.

**Things to Look For**

Talk of planning an event. You may overhear someone speaking of planning an incident. Notify authorities and provide as much information as possible.

If someone shows an interest in the acquisition of explosives or other bomb making materials, they should be investigated further.

If you see someone in a sensitive area taking photos, using a video camera, sketching pictures or taking notes, they should be contacted, identified and documented.

Inquires about security procedures, staffing of businesses, location of surveillance cameras or other sensitive questions may be example of probing. Terrorists may be gathering operational information to plot an attack.

Possession or the active seeking of items inconsistent with someone's employment or hobby: Examples of this would include weapons, identification badges, uniforms, equipment, explosives or literature about the building of explosives.

Be aware of people with known associations to fanatical groups or criminal organizations. Someone expressing an active interest in these types of groups should be of concern.

It's possible that information of these types could be obtained during traffic stops, pedestrian checks or other "routine" contacts. It's critical that officers maintain a high level of vigilance.

## Reporting

Encourage the public to call 911 if they have concerns about a suspicious act. If it is not urgent, be sure to offer non-emergency contact numbers or anonymous tip lines.

## Suspicious Packages

Terrorists occasionally have used the mail system or other delivery services to further their criminal acts. You encounter a call where someone has received a suspicious package.

Do not open a suspicious package if you see protruding wires, oily stains, powdery substances felt through an envelope, or if you hear a ticking sound. Other suspicious indicators may include a package with excessive postage, a poorly typed or badly handwritten address, incorrect spelling of common words, strange return address or mail not addressed to a specific person.

When checking a suspicious package, do not shake or empty the contents. Put the package down in a secure location. Do not carry it around to show others, but do alert others in the area of the potential hazard. Minimize your exposure. Do not sniff, taste, touch or examine the contents. Do not use a cell phone or 2 way radio near the package. Use of these devices can emit signals that may cause explosives to detonate.

If you have handled a package with an unknown residue or powder, wash your hands immediately with soap and water. Notify a bomb squad, haz-mat unit or fire agency immediately.

## Types of Terrorism

**Agro Terrorism**: This is the act of tampering with or damaging the food supply through the use malicious use of pathogens to cause disease.

**Bio Terrorism**: Bio terrorism is the intentional release of germs, biological materials, viruses, bacteria or other agents used to cause death or illness in humans, animals or plants.

**Domestic Terrorism**: Terrorist acts committed by an American citizen against American targets.

**Cyber Terrorism:** Cyber terrorists use computer resources to intimidate or coerce others by causing problems. They may hack into computer networks causing dangerous changes. They can digitally steal funds, information or identities without the owner's knowledge. As computer technology becomes more common in our society, this problem grows along with it. Prosecution of these crimes is often difficult because the suspects can be spread around the world.

**Eco Terrorism**: The FBI defines eco terror as the use or threatened use of violence of a criminal nature against people or property by an environmentally oriented, subnational group for environmental or political reasons, or aimed at an audience beyond the target, often of a symbolic nature. Eco terrorists often target people or businesses who commit cruelty to animals or damage to the environment through construction or industrialization.

**International Terrorism**: Acts committed around the globe by various terrorist groups crossing international borders. Attacks are often based on disagreements over foreign policy or beliefs.

**Narco Terrorism:** Terrorism where there is a connection between drug traffickers and international terrorists. Drug dealers often sell drugs to finance terrorist operations.

**State Sponsored Terrorism:** Non-military personnel who are committing terrorist acts under the direction of a formal structured national government.

**Religious Terrorism:** Terrorists who use violence under the theory that the beliefs of their chosen religion are the rule. Anyone who deviates from the beliefs should be destroyed.

## Workplace / School Violence

Violence at schools and in the workplace should not be taken lightly. Acts of violence at schools and in the workplace can often be considered acts of terrorism. Monitor the behavior of students or employees and watch for abnormal things. Disgruntled persons often speak freely about bad things they would like to do. Some may only be joking, but all threats need to be addressed, even if they are minor.

Schools and business should have emergency plans in place should an incident occur. Both workplaces and schools should have written policies stating what violence is and that it will not be tolerated. Terrorism is a crime of opportunity. Remain observant, document all concerns and do all you can to reduce the opportunities for a terrorist to be successful. Staff, students or employees should all be trained on what to do, should violence occur.

School administrators and students should be encouraged to notify authorities immediately when something out of the ordinary is observed. If someone is actively showing signs of aggression, remain calm. Try to defuse the situation by calmly reasoning with the person. Good communication skills can often de-escalate situations.  If the anger escalates, call for back up immediately. Schools and businesses should have an evacuation or lock down plan in place should a violent incident occur.

If an employee is terminated in the workplace, extra vigilance should be shown. If threats are made, you must take them seriously. Try to prevent problems before they escalate into something larger.

# Disease Outbreaks / Biological Attacks

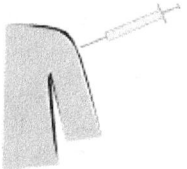

Diseases are around us every day. Some diseases can spread rapidly, sometimes turning into a pandemic. A pandemic is an infectious disease outbreak that spreads through human populations across a large region or worldwide. Recent outbreaks have included the H1N1 virus (also known as Swine Flu), Avian Influenza (Bird Flu) and SARS (Severe Acute Respiratory Syndrome). Though you can't prevent disease outbreaks, you can do some things to minimize the effects.

Be aware of disease warnings. If vaccinations are available, you should consider getting one. Influenza, also known as "the flu" is the most common virus spread among humans. It affects thousands of people each year. The elderly and young children are the most vulnerable. Flu shots are available year round, but they are often in short supply as flu season nears (late fall). Symptoms of the flu may include: fever, runny or stuffy nose, chills, headaches or body aches and fatigue.

The best way to prevent the spread of viruses is to limit your exposure to those who are infected. Avoid contact with items handled by those who may be sick. Sanitize things such as telephones, computer keyboards, and toys. When you are infected, don't share cups, glasses or silverware without properly washing them first. Clean and sanitize bathrooms, door knobs, light switches or anything else that may have been touched. If you are coughing or sneezing, stay home until you show no symptoms for at least 24 hours. Most importantly wash your hands with soap and water after shaking hands, or touching items that may be contaminated. If you don't have access to soap and water, carry a bottle of sanitizer with you in your duty bag or patrol car. They are very inexpensive and can kill many germs.

.

## Biological Agents as Weapons

Biological agents are organisms or toxins that can kill or incapacitate people, livestock, and crops. Biological agents can be used as weapons. The three basic groups of biological agents that could be used are bacteria, viruses, and toxins. Most biological agents are difficult to grow and maintain. Many break down quickly when exposed to sunlight and other environmental factors, while others, such as anthrax spores live for a long time. A biological attack may not be immediately obvious. Symptoms may start showing up days or even weeks after a release. Medical assistance may not be immediately available. The cause of the illness may not be known and it may take time to determine a treatment.

In the event of a known incident, listen to the media for official instructions. If a biological attack were to occur, be sure to follow the instructions provided by the media. The decision to evacuate or shelter in place will depend on the location and intensity of the attack.

If you encounter an unknown or suspicious substance, you should move away quickly and contact the appropriate authorities. Seek medical attention if you become ill.

If you come into contact with unknown or suspicious substance, wash with soap and water immediately. If your clothing or other items are infected, remove them are securely bag them. Seek medical attention for full decontamination.

## Pathogen Delivery Methods

**Aerosols** - Biological agents are dispersed into the air, forming a fine mist that may drift for miles. Inhaling the agent may cause disease in people or animals.

**Powders**: Spores such as anthrax can be spread through powders. These powders can be inhaled or absorbed through the skin when touched causing illness.

**Animals**: Some diseases can spread by insects and animals. Insects can carry disease, which can then infect humans and animals when bitten. You can minimize insect infestation by draining standing water and maintaining a sanitary area. Wear insect repellent or protective clothing when outside in high risk areas.

**Food and water contamination**: Some pathogenic organisms and toxins may persist in food and water supplies. Most microbes can be killed, and toxins deactivated, by properly cooking food and boiling water. Most microbes are killed by boiling water for one minute, but some require longer. Keep counter tops clean that are used for food preparation.

**Explosives**: Toxins may also be spread through the use of explosive dispersion.

**Human Contact** (person-to-person): This is the easiest way to spread germs. Germs can be spread by physical contact, or airborne methods such as coughing or sneezing. Avoiding contact with sick people and frequently washing your hands are the best prevention for the spread of germs. Waterless hand sanitizers are also effective. If you are entering an environment where you know there is a chance of contamination, wear a protective mask or respirator.

## HEPA Filters

High Efficiency Particulate Air (HEPA) filters are useful tools in biological attacks as well as maintaining the air quality in your home or office. If you have a central heating and cooling system that uses a HEPA filter, leave it on if it is running or turn the fan on if it is not running. Circulating the air in the house through the filter will help to remove particulates from the air. Portable HEPA filters can be moved into your safe room to help clean the air.

**Note: HEPA filters will not filter chemical agents.**

# Chapter 9

# Resources

## American Red Cross

The American Red Cross is a volunteer organization that has been providing invaluable disaster relief support since 1881. They assist with food, lodging and other immediate needs during and after a disaster. In addition to domestic disaster relief, the American Red Cross offers compassionate services in five other areas: community services that help the needy; support and comfort for military members and their families; the collection, processing and distribution of lifesaving blood and blood products; educational programs that promote health and safety such as CPR and first aid classes; and international relief and development programs.

The Red Cross operates nearly 700 locally supported chapters in the United States. Whether it's around the corner or around the world, the Red Cross is there to help. The Red Cross is also the largest supplier of blood and blood products in the United States. Over four million people donate blood to the Red Cross each year. They collect and distribute roughly half of the blood supply in the United States.

## Community Emergency Response Team (CERT)

The CERT program supports local emergency response capabilities by allowing trained volunteers to assist with disasters. This is the modern version of civil defense as it was once known. CERT teams can provide immediate emergency assistance to victims if other rescuers are not available.

CERT trainings are often presented by local government agencies or other authorized representatives. The classroom training courses provides 20 hours of specialized disaster preparedness instruction.

CERT training educates participants about potential hazards faced in a disaster. Content also includes training on search and rescue, fire safety, disaster medical operations, organizational skills and disaster psychology.

After completing CERT training, participants are encouraged to get involved with community events and training activities that support emergency preparedness.

**Citizen Corps**

Citizen Corps is a federal program that provides opportunities for people across the country to participate in a wide range of activities to make their families, homes, and communities safer. Through public education, training opportunities, and volunteer programs, "every American can do their part to be better prepared and better protected and to help their communities do the same".

Citizen Corps is managed at the local level by Citizen Corps Councils, which bring together leaders from law enforcement, fire, emergency medical and other emergency management, volunteer organizations, local elected officials, the private sector, and other community stakeholders.

These Citizen Corps Councils organize public education on disaster mitigation and preparedness, citizen training, and volunteer programs to give people of all ages and backgrounds the opportunity to support emergency services in their community and to safeguard themselves and their property.

**Medical Reserve Corps**

If you have experience and skills as a nurse, doctor or other form of medical professional, you can sign up for the Medical Reserve Corps. This is an organization of professionals who are ready to respond to disasters to provide medical assistance. Specific skills are needed to participate with this organization and travel is often required.

## National Fire Corps

Fire Corps volunteers assist local fire and emergency service departments with administrative duties, special programs and life safety education and other services.

## Radio Amateur Civil Emergency Service (RACES)

RACES volunteers are trained amateur radio operators. They offer emergency communications services that can called upon in times of need. This is a vital service that utilizes amateur radio frequencies. In a major disaster, this may be the only communications available. To find out more about how you can get involved with RACES, contact your local emergency management office.

## Volunteer Fire Fighting

There are many fire departments across the nation that offer volunteer firefighting opportunities. Training is usually provided by the department, but you can also receive certifications at local community colleges.

## Volunteers in Police Service

The demands on law enforcement agencies have increased dramatically in recent years. With budgets being cut further than ever, staffing resources are limited. At a time when police agencies need every available certified officer on patrol, resources can be stretched thin.

Volunteers can work with a law enforcement agency in a variety of roles. Tasks may include serving as an extra pair of eyes and ears on the street, search and rescue, administrative duties, or other services based on your skills. You can also serve part time as a reserve or auxiliary officer if you meet certain qualifications. Contact your local law enforcement agency for more information.

## Other Groups

There are also many private and faith based organizations that provide disaster relief services. Check your local area to find out who offers these services and how you can get involved.

If you have an interest in extreme weather, becoming a storm spotter or storm chaser may be of interest to you. To find out more about how to become certified as storm spotter, contact your local emergency management office or the National Weather Service office in your area. Courses are usually free and are offered several times a year. You can also find information on the internet or at your local library.

## Neighborhood Watch

Organize or get involved with a neighborhood watch group. The police can't be everywhere, so more eyes and ears in your neighborhoods can increase safety. Neighborhood Watch is a great way to help make your community a better place to live. Police and residents need to work together to reduce crime.

## Stay Informed

Monitor news and weather reports. Be aware of current events and potential hazards. Seek further training.

## Educate Others

Spread the word about safety and preparedness. Encourage your churches, schools, businesses, or other organizations to host a seminar on safety and emergency planning. Encourage your agency to host a "safety day" let the public meet responders.

# Chapter 10

## Disaster / Weather Terminology

To better understand a disaster, you should know the terminology. You may have heard some of these terms used while watching the news or listening to warnings. Each term has definitions included.

**Accumulation** - The actual measurable depth of any precipitation on the ground during a given time period.

**Advisory** - Issued by the National Weather Service to highlight weather conditions that require caution, but are not thought to be immediately life threatening.

**Al Qaeda** – A terrorist organization that opposes non-Islamic governments.

**Air Pollution** – Chemicals or substances in the atmosphere that are directly or indirectly harmful to living things.

**Air Pressure** - Weight of the air pressing down on the Earth. It is also known as barometric pressure.

**Anemometer** - A weather instrument used to measure wind speed.

**Arctic Air** - Air masses that originate over Canada bringing cold temperatures south.

**Atmosphere** - A layer of gases surrounding a planet. The Earth's atmosphere is divided into five layers: exosphere, thermosphere, mesosphere, stratosphere, and troposphere.

**Aurora Borealis** - Often called the "Northern Lights", they occur when energetic particles from a solar storm cause the gases in the upper atmosphere to glow.

**Avalanche** - A large body of snow, ice or rock and debris sliding down a mountain or hillside.

**Barometer** - An instrument that measures air pressure.

**Barometric Pressure** - The pressure exerted by the atmosphere, also known as air pressure.

**Beaufort Wind Scale** - A system of estimating and reporting wind speeds. It is based on the Beaufort Force or Number, which is composed of the wind speed, a descriptive term, and the visible effects upon land objects and/or sea surfaces. The scale was devised by Sir Francis Beaufort (1777-1857), a hydrographer and officer for the British Royal Navy.

**Bermuda High** - It's a weather system that often dominates the eastern United States during the summer. A semi-permanent subtropical high-pressure system over the North Atlantic Ocean brings in warm and humid air for many days or weeks at a time. It gets its name because it is sometimes centered near Bermuda. It contributes to U.S. heat waves when it extends west into the Gulf of Mexico and across the Deep South.

**Blizzard** - An intense winter storm with winds of 35 mph or higher with falling and/or blowing snow that reduces visibility to below 1/4 mile for at least three hours. Blizzards can also have extremely cold temperatures.

**Blowing Snow Advisory** - When wind driven snow reduces surface visibility, it can cause dangerous driving conditions. Blowing snow may be falling snow or snow that has already accumulated on the ground but is picked up and blown by strong winds.

**Breeze** - A light wind.

**Car Bomb** – A vehicle filled with explosives.

**Ceiling** - The height of the lowest layer of broken or overcast cloud layer.

**CIA** – Abbreviation for the Central Intelligence Agency.

**Climate** - The average weather conditions in a certain place or during a certain season.

**Clouds** - A visible collection of water or frozen ice crystals suspended in the air above the surface.

**Coastal Flooding** - When winds and/or tides create a rise in the sea level that causes flooding in coastal areas.

**Coastal Flood Warning** - Land areas along the coast are expected to become, or have become, inundated by sea water above the typical tide action.

**Coastal Flood Watch** - The possibility exists for the inundation of land areas along the coast within the next 12 to 36 hours.

**Cold Front** - A boundary between two air masses, one cold and the other warm, moving so that the colder air replaces the warmer air.

**Condensation** - The change of water vapor to liquid water, as when fog or dew forms.

**Coriolis Force** - A force that deflects moving objects to one side because of the Earth's rotation.

**Cumulonimbus Clouds** - A dense and vertically developed cloud that produces thunderstorms. The cloud can bring heavy showers, hail, lightning, high winds and sometimes tornadoes.

**Cumulus Clouds** – Large, towering fluffy clouds

**Cyclone** - A term variously applied to tornadoes, waterspouts, dust storms and hurricanes.

**Dense Fog** - Fog that reduces horizontal visibility to 1/4 mile or less.

**Dense Fog Advisory** - Issued when dense fog covers a widespread area and reduces visibility to ¼ of a mile or less.

**Dew** - Water that forms on objects close to the ground when its temperature falls below the dew point of the surface air.

**Dew Point** - The temperature at which water starts to condense out of a particular air mass. The dew point temperature changes only when the moisture content of the air changes. The higher the dew point, the greater the moisture content is in the air.

**DHS** – Abbreviation for the Department of Homeland Security, a federal agency tasked with protecting the United States against terrorism.

**Dirty Bomb** – A conventional explosive device created with radioactive material.

**Disturbance** - A low pressure system, a tropical area of storminess, or any area in which the weather is in a state of cloudiness, precipitation or wind.

**Downburst** - A strong downward rush of air, which produces a blast of damaging winds on or close to the surface.

**Drizzle** - Light rain consisting of water droplets that are very small.

**Drought** - An extended period of no rainfall.

**Dust Devil** - Small whirlwinds of dust that form in dry areas such as deserts. They are caused by swirling winds that rise with the warm air found over the ground.

**Earthquake** - The shaking or movement of a portion of the Earth's surface caused by fault movement.

**El Niño** - The unusual warming of the surface waters of the eastern tropical Pacific Ocean. It causes changes in wind patterns that have major effects on weather all across the globe. It is the opposite of La Niña.

**EMS** – Abbreviation for Emergency Medical Service

**EMT** – Abbreviation for Emergency Medical Technician

**Enhanced Fujita Scale** – A scale used to measure the intensity of tornadoes based on the amount damage caused. **Also see Fujita Scale.** Scale is based on wind speed/damage.

EF-0: Winds 65 - 85 mph
EF-1: Winds 86 - 109 mph
EF-2: Winds: 110 - 137 mph
EF-3: Winds 138 – 167 mph
EF-4: Winds 168 – 199 mph
EF-5: Winds 200 – 234 mph

**Environment** - The surroundings of a person, place or thing.

**EOD** – Abbreviation for Explosive Ordinance Disposal, another name for a police, fire or military "bomb squad". EOD teams assist with the removal and disposal of explosive devices.

**Erosion** - The wearing away of the Earth's surface by the action of moving water, ice, precipitation or wind.

**Evaporation** - The process of a liquid changing to a vapor.

**Excessive Heat Warning** - Issued within 12 hours of the onset of the heat conditions listed in the excessive heat watch.

**Excessive Heat Watch** - Issued when the following conditions occur within 12-36 hours: a heat index of at least 105 degrees for more than 3 hours per day for 2 consecutive days or a heat index more than 115 degrees for any period of time.

**Fahrenheit** – The scale most commonly used for weather temperature measurement in the United States. It is abbreviated as °F. Using the Fahrenheit scale, the freezing point of water is 32°F and the boiling point is 212°F.

**Fallout** – Radioactive particles falling from the sky after a radiological release.

**Fault** - A planar fracture or discontinuity in a volume of rock across which there has been significant displacement. The movement of faults in the ground causes earthquakes.

**Farmer's Almanac** - A calendar that lists tide data, gives     the positions of the stars and forecasts weather for a year in advance.

**FBI** – Abbreviation for the Federal Bureau of Investigation,     a US agency tasked with domestic law enforcement.

**FEMA** – Abbreviation for the Federal Emergency Management Agency

**Flash Flood** - A rapid and extreme flow of high water into a normally dry area, or a rapid water level rise in a stream or creek above a predetermined flood level, beginning within six hours of a weather event.

**Flash Flood Watch** - Issued when conditions exist that could cause rapid flooding in low lying areas or in locations where the ground is already saturated from recent rains.

**Flash Flood Warning** - Issued when rapid flooding is in progress or is imminent in watch areas.

**Flood** – An expanse of water that submerges land.

**Flood Plain** – Flat areas bordering rivers or streams that experience periodic or occasional flooding.

**Flood Stage** - The level at which a stream, river or other body of water will begin to overflow its banks.

**Fog** - A cloud on the ground that reduces visibility.

**Freeze** - When temperatures fall below 32 degrees for an extended period of time.

**Freeze Warning** - Issued when temperatures are expected to fall below 32 degrees for an extended period of time.

**Freezing Rain** - Rain that falls in liquid form but freezes upon impact to form a coating of glaze on surfaces.

**Front** - A boundary between two different air masses, resulting in stormy weather. A front usually is a line of separation between warm and cold air masses.

**Frost** - Formed when solid surfaces are cooled to below the dew point of the surrounding air and below the freezing point of water.

**Frost Advisory** - Issued when a widespread frost is expected over an extensive area.

**Frostbite** – A damaging medical condition that occurs when skin is exposed to excessive cold.

**F Scale** – See Fujita scale

**Fujita Scale** - The traditional scale used to measure the strength of tornadoes based upon wind speed. The scale ranges from F0 (lowest) to F5 (highest). Meteorologists are now often using the **Enhanced Fujita** scale measurement.

**F0**: winds 40-72 mph - (Light damage)
Branches can be broken off trees.

**F1**: winds 73-112 mph - (Moderate damage)
Trees snap and mobile home can be pushed off foundations.

**F2**: winds 113-157 mph - (Considerable damage)
Mobile homes demolished and trees uprooted.

**F3**: winds 158-206 mph - (Severe damage)
Trains can be overturned and cars lifted off the ground.

**F4**: winds 207-260 mph - (Devastating damage)
Houses leveled and cars thrown some distance.

**F5**: winds 261-318 mph - (Incredible damage)
Houses may be lifted and thrown some distance.

**Funnel Cloud** – A rotating column of air extending downward from the base of a cumulonimbus or thunderstorm cloud, not making contact with the ground.

**Glacier** - A large mass of ice that moves over land.

**Glaze** - A coating of ice, usually clear and smooth, formed on exposed objects by the freezing of rain, drizzle, or fog.

**Global Warming** - The theory that increased concentrations of greenhouse gases are causing the surface temperature of the Earth to rise.

**Gulf Stream** - A warm swift current in the Atlantic Ocean that flows from the Gulf of Mexico along the eastern coast of the United States northeast toward Europe.

**Hail** – Rain drops inside cumulonimbus clouds are forced upward in the cloud by updrafts, gathering moisture as they rise. As layers of ice form, they will become heavy and will fall from the sky in the form of balls other irregular shapes known as hail stones.

**Hard Freeze** -When the air temperature is expected to be 26 degrees or colder for at least 4 consecutive hours.

**Haze** - Tiny particles of dust, smoke, salt or pollution droplets that are scattered through the air.

**Haz-Mat** – Abbreviation for Hazardous Materials

**Heat Advisory** - Issued within 12 hours of the onset of the following conditions: a heat index of at least 105 degrees but less than 115 degrees for less than 3 hours per day or if nighttime lows remain above 80 degrees for 2 consecutive days.

**Heat Index** - The "feel like" temperature on a hot day when you combine humidity with the actual air temperature.

**Heat Lightning** - Heat lightning is just lightning that is too far away for its thunder to be heard.

**Heavy Snow Warning** - Issued when snowfall totaling 6 inches or more in 12 hours or less is expected. Also issued when there is 8 inches or more of snow expected in 24 hours or less.

**High Pressure System** - Mass of warm, dry air that generally brings nice weather.

**High Wind Warning** - Issued when winds of 40 mph or greater are occurring or expected to occur for at least one hour. It also occurs if winds of 58 mph or greater are expected.

**High Wind Watch** - Issued when conditions are favorable of the development of high winds.

**Humidity** - The amount of water vapor in the air.

**Hurricane** - Intense storms with swirling winds up to 150 mph. usually around 300 miles across, hurricanes are 1,000-5,000 times larger than tornadoes.

**Hurricane Season** - The six-month period from June 1 to Nov. 30, when conditions are favorable for hurricane development.

**Hygrometer** - An instrument that measures humidity.

**Ice** - Water in a solid phase. Water becomes ice when it is cooled below 32 degrees (F) or 0 degrees(C).

**Iceberg** – A chunk of freshwater ice that has broken off a glacier and is floating in open water.

**Ice Storms** - They occur when temperatures below a rain cloud are very cold, causing the raindrops to become super cooled (less than 32 degrees Fahrenheit).

**Ice Storm Warning** - Issued when damaging accumulations of ice are expected during a freezing rain event.

**ICS** – Incident Command System

**IED** – Abbreviation for an Improvised Explosive Device.

**Indian Summer** – Warm weather in the autumn.

**Inversion** - A layer in the atmosphere where the temperature increases with height.

**Jet Stream** - A strong high level wind found in the atmosphere that can reach speeds in excess of 200 mph, usually occurring 6 to 9 miles above the ground. These winds often steer the movement of surface air masses and weather systems.

**La Niña** - A widespread cooling of the surface waters of the eastern tropical Pacific Ocean. It's the opposite of El Niño.

**Lake Effect Snow** - Localized snow that forms on the downwind side of large lakes. It's common in the late fall and winter in the Great Lakes region when cold, dry air picks up moisture from the unfrozen lake surfaces.

**Lightning** – An atmospheric discharge of electricity produced during thunderstorms.

**Low Pressure System** - A cool dry air mass that often brings cooler weather, and storms.

**Macroburst** - A large down draft of air with an outflow diameter of at least 2.5 miles and damaging winds lasting about 5 to 20 minutes.

**Microburst** - A small downdraft of air with an outflow diameter of less than 2.5 miles with peak winds lasting from 2 to 5 minutes.

**Meteor** – Sometimes called a "shooting star", it is a rock made of composite material falling from space.

**Meteor Shower** - When hundreds of meteors can be seen in the sky at the same time.

**Meteorite** - A meteor that reaches the Earth's surface.

**Meteorologist** - A scientist who studies and predicts the weather.

**Meteorology** - The study of the atmosphere and all its phenomena, including weather and how to forecast it.

**Mist** – Very small water droplets floating in the air.

**MPH** – Abbreviation for Miles per Hour, a measure of speed.

**Monsoon** - A seasonal wind, occurring in Asia that reverses direction between summer and winter. It often brings heavy rains. It also refers to heavy seasonal rains in the southwest United States.

**Muggy** - The description of warm and humid air.

**National Hurricane Center** - They issue watches, warnings, forecasts, and analyses of hazardous tropical weather.

**National Weather Service** – The federal agency that provides climate forecasts and weather warnings for the United States.

**Nexrad** – Abbreviation for the "NEXt generation weather RADar", a nationwide network of 120 Doppler radars used by the National Weather Service to monitor weather conditions.

**NIMS** – Abbreviation for the National Incident Management System, a US national emergency response plan.

**Nor'easter** - A powerful low-pressure system that moves along the Atlantic Coast. It's called a Nor'easter because the coastal winds come from the northeast. Heavy rain, snow and high tides often occur.

**Overcast** - Widespread layers of clouds covering the sky.

**Ozone** - Ozone is a form of oxygen that heats the upper atmosphere by absorbing ultraviolet light from sunlight. In the troposphere, ozone is a pollutant, but in the stratosphere it filters out harmful ultraviolet radiation.

**Ozone Warning** – If an ozone warning is issued, it means air quality is poor. People with respiratory issues such as asthma should limit outdoor physical activity.

**Pathogen** – Any agent that can cause disease.

**Precipitation** - General name for any water form, falling from clouds.

**Radar** - An electronic instrument which determines the direction and distance of objects that reflect radio energy back to the radar site. Radar is used to detect hazardous weather.

**Rain** - Liquid precipitation in the form of water drops that fall from clouds.

**Rain Gauge** - An instrument used to measure the amount of rain that has fallen. Measurement is done in hundredths of inches (0.01").

**Relative Humidity** - The ratio of water vapor contained in the air compared to the maximum amount of moisture that the air can hold at that specific temperature and pressure.

**Saffir-Simpson Scale** - A hurricane intensity scale used to relate hurricane damage to wind speed and central air pressures.

**Category 1**: wind speeds 74-95 mph
**Category 2**: wind speeds 96-110 mph
**Category 3**: wind speeds 111-130 mph
**Category 4**: wind speeds 131-155 mph
**Category 5**: wind speeds over 155 mph

The scale also measures the intensity of storm surges (rising sea water levels)

**Sandstorm** - Strong winds in dry desert regions can carry large amounts sand or dirt through the air. A wall of dirt or sand, sometimes a mile high or wide can resemble a storm as it moves through. They are also referred to as dust storms.

**Severe Thunderstorm** - Thunderstorms with winds of 58 mph or greater and/or with hail ¾ inch in diameter or larger.

**Severe Thunderstorm Warning** - Issued when a severe thunderstorm is forecast to occur or is occurring. The warning will include where the storm was occurring, its direction of movement and the primary threat from the storm.

**Severe Thunderstorm Watch** - Issued when conditions are favorable for the development of severe thunderstorms.

**Severe Weather** - Any weather event that could possibly be life threatening, or could cause damage.

**Showers** – Falling rain in scattered areas.

**Shear** - A variation in wind speed and/or direction.

**Sleet** - Solid precipitation in the form of ice pellets form when raindrops, originating in warmer air aloft, freeze as they fall through subfreezing air near the surface of the Earth.

**Sleet Warning** - Issued when accumulations of sleet in excess of a half inch are expected.

**Slush** - Snow or ice on the ground that has been reduced to a soft, watery mixture by rain or warm temperatures.

**Small Craft Advisory** - A warning issued by the National Weather Service most frequently in coastal areas. It is issued when winds have reached, or are expected to reach within 12 hours, a speed marginally less than that which is considered gale force, usually 25-38 mph.

**Smog** - Visible air pollution in urban areas. Smog is formed from smoke and vehicle exhaust.

**Snow** - Precipitation composed of white ice crystals falling from clouds. Snow is formed when water vapor in the air is less than 32 degrees (F).

**Snow Advisory** - Issued when snowfall is expected to exceed 2 inches but no more than 5 inches.

**Snow Drift** – Snow blown by winds that result in increased or uneven accumulations.

**Snow Flurries** - Brief occurrences of very light snow, producing little or no accumulation.

**Snow Showers** - Brief occurrences of light or moderate snow, which could produce some light accumulations.

**Squall Line** - A line of thunderstorms sometimes several hundred miles long that can produce strong thunderstorms and sometimes severe weather.

**Stable Air** - Air that is colder than its surroundings and is resistant to upward movement.

**Stationary Front** - A boundary between two air masses that remains stable.

**Storm** - Any disturbed state of the atmosphere that causes unpleasant weather conditions.

**Storm Chaser** – A storm chaser is a person who follows tornadoes or other severe weather as a hobby or for research purposes. They often try to get as close as possible to the weather hazard to photograph or document the severity.

**Storm Spotter** – A person specially trained in the detection, observation and reporting of severe weather. Spotters report information to the National Weather Service so warnings can be issued.

**Super Cell** - A severe thunderstorm where updrafts and down drafts are in near balance for several hours. Super Cells often produce large hail and tornadoes.

**Temperature** - The measurement of how hot or cold something is.

**Terrorism** – The use of unlawful violence or threat of unlawful violence to induce fear; intended to coerce or to intimidate governments or societies in the pursuit of goals that are generally political, religious, or ideological.

**Terrorist** – A person engaged in the act of terrorism.

**Thermometer** - An instrument used for measuring temperature.

**Thunder** - The explosive sound of air expanding as it is heated by lightning.

**Tidal Wave** – A large wave of water that can cause damage as it comes ashore.

**Tornado Warning** - Issued when a tornado is expected to occur, or is occurring. The warning will include where the storm was occurring and where it is expected to travel.

**Tornado Watch** - Issued when conditions are favorable for the development of tornadoes.

**Tornado Alley** – Area of the central United States where tornadoes occur most frequently.

**Tropical Storm** - Low pressure disturbances that form in the area over warm tropical ocean waters. Tropical storms typically have winds between 39-73 mph. Tropical storms can progress into hurricanes.

**Tropical Depression** - Low pressure disturbances that form in the area over warm tropical ocean water. Wind speeds are 38 mph or less. Tropical depressions can progress into tropical storms.

**Troposphere** - The lowest portion of Earth's atmosphere where weather occurs.

**TSA** – Abbreviation for the Transportation Security Agency, a federal agency tasked with the protection of US transportation facilities.

**Tsunami** – A Japanese term for an unusually large ocean wave caused by undersea earthquake, landslide, or volcanic eruption.

**Typhoon** - A hurricane in the western Pacific Ocean.

**Unstable Air** - Air that is warmer than its surroundings and tends to rise, leading to the formation of clouds and precipitation.

**Virga** - Rain or snow that falls from a cloud but evaporates before it reaches the ground.

**Visibility** - The greatest distance possible for a person to see with their eyes.

**Volcano** - Any place where lava, ash or volcanic gases escape to the surface of the Earth.

**Wall Cloud** - Area of clouds that extends underneath a thunderstorm.

**Warm Front** - The boundary between two air masses, one cool and the other warm, moving so the warmer air replaces the cooler air.

**Warning** - A forecast issued by the National Weather Service indicating that a specific weather event is actually occurring.

**Watch** - A forecast issued by the National Weather Service indicating that conditions are favorable for a particular weather hazard.

**Waterspout** - A tornado occurring over water.

**Whiteout** – Occurs during extreme blizzard conditions when blowing snow or falling snow reduces visibility so the sky, air, and ground becomes indistinguishable.

**Wildfire** – A fire in grassy or forested areas that burns out of control. Wildfires can be caused naturally by lightning or by humans, accidentally or intentionally.

**WMD** – Abbreviation for Weapons of Mass Destruction

**Wind** – Movement of air relative to the surface of the earth.

**Wind Advisory** - An advisory from the National Weather Service when winds are expected to be between 29-38 mph, lasting more than one hour, or when wind gusts are expected to be between 44-57 mph.

**Wind Chill** - The "feel like" temperature when you factor in wind speed with temperature.

**Wind Chill Factor** - A number that expresses the cooling effect of moving air at different temperatures. Air temperature and wind speed is used in the calculation of wind chill temperatures.

**Wind Chill Advisory** - Issued when winds of 10 mph or greater are expected to create wind chill factors of 30 degrees below zero or more.

**Winter Storm Warning** - Issued when hazardous winter weather is occurring. Hazardous winter weather includes heavy snows, blizzards, ice storms, freezing rain, freezing drizzle and sleet.

**Winter Storm Watch** – A watch is issued when there is a potential for heavy snow or significant ice accumulations, usually at least 24 to 36 hours in advance.

**Winter Weather Advisory** - The National Weather Service issues these advisories when a low pressure system produces a combination of winter weather (snow, freezing rain, sleet, etc.) that can present a hazard, but does not meet warning criteria.

**WX** – Abbreviation for weather.

## About the Author

Marty Augustine is a veteran law enforcement officer and a nationally known safety educator. He travels the US presenting his **Responding to Disaster** seminar which features content from this book. Marty encourages patrol officers to become more efficient and effective emergency responders.

**For more information, visit his website:**
www.MartyAugustine.com

**He can also be contacted at the address below.**

Marty Augustine
P.O. Box 3091
Shawnee, KS 66203

**Other Books by Marty Augustine:**

**At Ground Zero** (An Emergency Preparedness Guide)

**Success: They Have It, Why Can't I**

## Resource Contact Information

**American Red Cross National Headquarters**
2025 E Street, NW
Washington, DC 20006
Website: www.REDCROSS.org

**Civilian Volunteer Medical Reserve Corps**
Office of the Surgeon General
U.S. Department of Health and Human Services
5600 Fishers Lane, Room 18C-14
Rockville, MD 20857
Website: www.MEDICALRESERVECORPS.gov

**The National Office of Citizen Corps**
**FEMA Individual and Community Preparedness Div.**
Techworld Building, 800 K. Street NW
Suite 640, Washington, D.C. 20472-3630
Website:www.CITIZENCORPS.gov

**Federal Emergency Management Agency**
U.S. Department of Homeland Security
500 C Street SW, Washington, D.C. 20472
Website: www.FEMA.gov

**National Fire Corps**
7852 Walker Drive, Suite 450
Greenbelt, MD 20770
Website: www.FIRECORPS.org

**Volunteers in Police Service Program**
International Association of Chiefs of Police
515 N. Washington St.
Alexandria, VA 22314
Website: www.POLICEVOLUNTEERS.org

All contact information was current at the time of publishing

## Additional Internet Resources

Center for Disease Control
www.CDC.gov

Central Intelligence Agency
www.CIA.gov

Department of Homeland Security
www.DHS.gov

Federal Bureau of Investigation
www.FBI.gov

US Geological Survey
www.USGS.gov

National Oceanic and Atmospheric Administration
www.NOAA.gov

National Security Agency
www.NSA.gov

National Weather Service
www.WEATHER.gov

Transportation Security Administration
www.TSA.gov

National Safety Council
www.NSC.org

Safe Kansas LLC
www.SafeKansas.com

This book is not endorsed or supported by any federal agency. Resources are included as references. The author and book have no direct affiliation with any of the agencies listed.

# Notes

www.ingramcontent.com/pod-product-compliance
Lightning Source LLC
Chambersburg PA
CBHW072311290526
45794CB00002B/611